THE ANGLING TIMES
BOOK OF THE SEVERN

The Angling Times
BOOK OF THE SEVERN

KEN COPE

DAVID & CHARLES
Newton Abbot   London   North Pomfret (Vt)
in association with
ANGLING TIMES

British Library Cataloguing in Publication Data

Cope, Ken
   The 'Angling Times' book of the Severn.
   1. Fishing – England – Severn River
   I. Title
   799.1'1'09424   SH606
   ISBN 0–7153–7791–4

Library of Congress Catalog Card Number: 79–51088

© EMAP National Publications Ltd 1979

Typeset by Trade Linotype Ltd,
and printed in Great Britain
by Biddles Limited, Guildford, Surrey
for David & Charles (Publishers) Limited
Brunel House Newton Abbot Devon

Published in the United States of America
by David & Charles Inc
North Pomfret Vermont 05053 USA

Contents

Introduction   7

Part 1: The River
The Three Reaches   11
The Severn in Flood   14

Part 2: Tackle and Bait
Tackle   21
Sliding Float   26
Bait   29

Part 3: Match Fishing
A Tough Test   37
Methods and Tactics   39

Part 4: The Fish
Barbel   47
Bleak   60
Bream   66
Chub   75
Dace   94
Eels and Elvers   100
Grayling   104
Pike   108
Roach   112
Salmon   121
Shad   126
Trout   128

Part 5: Where to Fish

Llanidloes to Caersws   133
Caersws to Newtown   136
Newtown to Welshpool   138
Welshpool to Shrewsbury   141
Shrewsbury to Atcham   144
Atcham to Cressage   148
Cressage to Bridgnorth   151
Bridgnorth to Hampton Loade   156
Hampton Loade to Bewdley   161
Bewdley to Stourport   166
Stourport to Holt Fleet   169
Holt Fleet to Worcester   171
Worcester to Upton-on-Severn   174
Upton-on-Severn to Tewkesbury   177
Tewkesbury to Gloucester.   180

Appendices

1 Licences   185
2 The Birmingham Anglers' Association   186
3 Clubs and Associations   188

Introduction

In this book I have endeavoured to describe every aspect, style and method of angling, related to the main fish species of the Severn which are barbel, bleak, bream, chub, dace, eels, grayling, roach, salmon and trout. Not forgetting the popular twaite shad, a rare saltwater visitor that provides excellent sport in the tidal reaches in the spring. I have not included perch for the simple reason that they are few in number, though it is pleasing to note that this fine fighting fish is returning slowly after being almost wiped out by disease. Neither have I bothered with gudgeon, that ubiquitous 'Little Samson' which thrives at many venues but for which no one, not even the matchman, angles seriously.

When describing the various methods, baits and tactics used on the river I have divided them among the various species, but often one method and bait will tempt different kinds of fish from a particular swim. For instance, I have employed the swimfeeder for barbel, but this popular gadget which has in recent years become the most widely used method on the river actually attracts all bottom feeders. The 'fine-and-far-off' waggler style is another case in point because, while I have applied it to caster fishing for chub and barbel, it also works well with other baits for other species.

When I began this book I set out to list the lessees or owners of virtually every meadow along both banks of the river, from the source to the sea. But I found this an impossible task and there are gaps here and there, mainly where the water is controlled by small clubs or private individuals. The reader will find that there are comparatively few day-ticket stretches, but most associations and many clubs with holdings are open for membership at very reasonable subscriptions, so there is plenty of water available. For instance the Birmingham AA lease or own outright scores of miles of both banks between Llanidloes and Gloucester and membership is available to anyone. Access points and car parks at most venues on the river are normally listed in club and association membership books and should always be used. The Severn flows through rich farmland and farmers do not take kindly to anglers walking on crops or driving across meadows. Many a coveted stretch has been lost through the carelessness of anglers, so always follow 'The Country Code'.

*   *   *

I doubt if any angler knows the Severn intimately all along its length, and I am no exception. Therefore I should like to thank all anglers, club and association officials, and the Severn-Trent Water Authority for their help in supplying information for this book. Also a special 'thank you' to the Birmingham Anglers' Association whose *Guide to Waters* handbook proved invaluable in sorting out boundaries.

Part 1
The River

The Three Reaches

I am sure that few anglers would argue with my claim that the River Severn is the best mixed coarse and game river in the country. Supporting almost every species of freshwater fish it offers a wealth of excellent fishing of all styles along its great length—220 miles from its source to where it enters the Bristol Channel. Like all rain-fed rivers the Severn can be split into three separate reaches—upper, middle and lower —each of a different character but blending into each other and with no marked boundaries. For the purpose of this book, however, I have chosen Shrewsbury and Worcester as the dividing lines for the three stretches.

The Severn begins its long journey to the sea on the slopes of Bryn Cras, one of the peaks of Plynlimon in North Wales within two miles of the source of that other great river—the Wye. Before the Ice Age, millions of years ago, it flowed in a short direct route due west into the Irish Sea, but fortunately for thousands of anglers, great masses of ice forced it to take its present lengthy course. At normal level, and when in the peak of condition, the Severn runs clear but with a glistening dark hue that appears almost black at a distance. But, acting as a drain for hundreds of square miles of countryside including the wet mountainous region from where it sprang, it is quick to rise and then it becomes cocoa-coloured. When swollen it rages along at almost twice its normal speed (a fast walking pace) sweeping aside trees and boulders with its great power.

For the first 15 miles or so the Severn is little more than a mountain torrent and trout stream as it races through steep-sided valleys down to Llanidloes, the first town on its banks. There it is joined by the Clywedog and Dulas, two of the many tributaries and feeders that boost its flow.

11

Rushing and tumbling through a rocky and boulder-strewn course 'Sabrina', as the Romans called it, leaves Llanidloes and gradually eases into its typical upper character—a series of fords, rapids, fast glides, steady straights and deep pools. Anglers who appreciate natural beauty delight in the upper Severn where magnificent scenery echoes to the bubbling cry of the curlew. The sight of great buzzards wheeling and hovering high in the sky also adds extra enjoyment to wonderful fishing.

At Caersws it zigzags and meanders down into Newtown, the next sizeable town on its route, where it begins to widen slightly. Still meandering but in larger sweeps and steadying at more frequent intervals, the Severn swathes through lush countryside and on to Welshpool, being joined before the town by the River Rhiw which runs in at Berriew on the left bank, and the Camlad—the only river that flows from England into Wales. Below Welshpool, at Melverley, the first major tributary—the Vyrnwy—almost doubles the volume of water in the Severn when it converges on the left bank.

With this extra boost the Severn forges onward towards Shrewsbury where it takes three huge loops above, around and below the town before rushing away to Atcham where the River Tern enters on the left bank. Long, steadier and deeper lengths now become more frequent but the fords, glides and shallow stretches continue to speed up the flow of the river.

This is the start of its middle stages which are more or less a grander version of the upper river. Onward across the Shropshire plain, past The Wrekin and falling 60ft in 21 miles, Sabrina is not easily turned aside now as it cuts through the Ironbridge Gorge and sweeps down majestically; wide in places, narrowing occasionally, deep-flowing and then shallow to Bridgnorth. Gravel-bottomed inches-deep fords, separated by smooth glides with mud-bottomed featureless straights, now give way to fast broken rapids with great slabs of sandstone which from time to time force the flow through channels and gullies, and there are fish everywhere.

We are now approaching some of the best and most popular venues on the river. So it continues through to Bewdley and to Blackstone Rock, the last ford on the river; from here on it steadies considerably with a much more even flow.

From Worcester downstream the Severn gradually enters into its third and lower stage, a wide, deep and powerful length of water with a strong, very even current. Below Worcester the River Teme converges on the right bank and its influence on the fishing, both good and bad, is felt as far down as Tewkesbury. Very deep stretches of up to 18ft are common along this reach. At Tewkesbury the River Avon runs in, and just below the confluence a weir marks the start of the tidal reaches. The tides have a marked effect on the river and all anglers in this area carry tide tables. Much shallower at low tide and wider than above Tewkesbury Weir, the Severn ploughs on to Gloucester where Llanthony Weir marks the beginning of the estuary. Because of the constant wash of the tides, the water is now heavily coloured and full of silt, making it unsuitable for fishing for anything other than eels.

The Severn in Flood

Great river that it is, the Severn has one failing that keeps anglers on tenter-hooks every week throughout the season, and that is its tendency to rise quickly. Sometimes it seems that the mere threat of rain in Wales is enough to raise the level a foot or so, and is it my imagination or do the frequent rises always come at weekends? But, as if extra water due to rain isn't enough to contend with, we are also dogged by regular influxes of dam water released from Lakes Vyrnwy and Clywedog, but more of that later.

Apart from the top end which stays remarkably clear when the river is in spate, the water becomes thick with sediment and the colour of milky tea. It is very turbulent, surging and 'boiling' as it races along and sport suffers as a consequence. Except for the barbel, which sometimes seem to revel in fresh water, fish become hard to find and difficult to catch in their usual haunts. It isn't that they do not feed in flood conditions, they do, at least in summer and autumn, it is just that they cannot see the bait, or we can't present it naturally because of the speed of the current. With, say three or so feet of extra water coursing through, the river runs extremely fast and the small fish have to seek the shelter of quieter or slower swims otherwise they would be washed away. The bigger species usually lie on or near the bottom and move very little, while barbel, with their great strength and bottom-hugging shape, are virtually unaffected and feed normally.

In these conditions float-fishing the stream is out of the question so it's a case of legering fairly close in, laying on, or easing a float down the side. Having said that, I must point out an exception, and that is when dace and roach move into shallow, clear-bottomed swims that are only inches

A typical winter scene on the river as an angler fishes a flood-swollen river at Winnalls

deep or dry at normal level. These areas often become nice steady glides when the river is up a few feet, and because of the discoloured water offer fishing at close range. One of the secrets of flood fishing is to offer a sizeable bait, one that the fish can find easily. Except for small fish in the quiet backwaters or lay-bys, single maggots or casters are almost useless in thick water. Bunches of three or four are more likely to attract reasonable-sized fish and these can be offered on a larger hook and stronger line than usual. Luncheon meat is an excellent bait for chub and barbel at any time but it really comes into its own when there is 'a drop on'. Sizeable lumps on a large size 4 or 6 hook have tempted many good bags of both species to win matches in poor conditions; and the fish are usually of a better stamp than are caught on a normal river.

The lobworm is another fine bait that scores in high water, which is not surprising as many are washed in by the floods

15

and fish come to expect them. Offer them singly or in doubles on a size 10 hook with a light rolling leger style, and if there are any fish around it is a safe bet the worm will be grabbed. Because of the surges and turbulence, feeding the deeper swims is a chancy business as groundbait (unless it is mixed really heavy), and loose offerings, are washed all over the place. The only safe way of putting maggots or casters on the bottom is to mix them in a putty-like ground-bait, or better still use a swimfeeder. This gadget is a great boon for floodwater and has accounted for many surprisingly big catches when other methods have proved useless. The only snag is that a lot of extra lead has to be added to anchor them down, which means that the rig becomes far too insensitive except for hard-pulling chub and barbel. The answer to this is to bait up with a feeder and then offer the hook bait with a light leger set up. Good catches of roach are taken using this dodge as well as big hauls of dace and other small fish.

When the Severn is unusually high and lapping its banks fishing of any description becomes almost impossible; but don't despair, just make for the confluence of one of the many brooks and streams that run into the river. Although quite shallow in normal conditions, these feeders fill up and become very deep and almost stationary against the push of the main river. In high floods they become calm havens and fish of all species swarm into them. An example of this is Hay Brook, below Bridgnorth. When the Severn is normal this stream averages about a foot deep, but at flood times I have known it back up to 16ft of virtually still water, full of roach, dace and chub. Other examples that spring to mind are the mouth of the River Tern at Atcham, Sheinton Brook at Cressage, the River Worfe above Bridgnorth, the Salwarpe at Bevere, Teme mouth below Worcester and the Mill Avon at Tewkesbury. All these tributaries and feeders, plus many more too numerous to list, offer good sport when the Severn is unfishable.

So far I have discussed natural flood conditions, but we are also plagued with unnatural rises due to millions of gallons of dam water being released at irregular intervals. Before Lake Clywedog was opened, the discharges came only from Lake Vyrnwy in two successive days each month. Vyrnwy water raised the level of the Severn less than a foot, but its effect all along the river was dramatic in that sport faded for days after it passed through. We accepted this regular interruption of our fishing however, putting it down to the fact that because the 'compensation water' as it was called came from the bottom of the lake it was de-oxygenated and cold which sickened the fish. But now we also have to contend with releases from Lake Clywedog and these seem to come at any old time, seemingly at the whim of the Water Authority's Engineering Department. There is a bone of contention between anglers and the Fisheries Department as to whether Clywedog discharges affect fishing.

In fact, an Authority scientist, Mr Rick North, has completed a two-year survey on the subject but unfortunately his results were not available at the time of writing. Mr North has pointed out though that during the drought of 1976 much of the Severn's flow consisted of dam water, yet fishing at most venues was first-class. While I agree that fishing was indeed excellent all through the drought, I believe it was only because the fish became accustomed to the dam water. I maintain, and I know that ninety-nine per cent of all Severn anglers would agree, that sudden influxes (except in hot weather when the effect is lessened) definitely put most species off feeding for a few days. It may be that Rick North's findings will show that we are wrong in our assumptions and that we blame dam water unnecessarily, but he will need a very strong argument to convince me.

Part 2
Tackle and Bait

Tackle

To make the most of the Severn's great sport potential the wise angler carries (or has available) a wide range of tackle suitable for the many different types of swims or species encountered. Of course, the specialist who seeks one or two particular species, or those anglers who confine their activities to a small stretch of the river (as many do) can get by with the basic essentials. But the all-rounders who fish the whole length of the river all the year round have enough gear to stock a small tackle shop. Which is hardly surprising as the Severn accommodates virtually every branch of the sport. Piking, eeling, salmon fishing, general coarse fishing, fly-fishing for trout or grayling . . . what more could an angler wish for.

Rods
In the rod department, I suppose the first choice must be a light 12ft to 13ft float rod which will be suitable for average run-of-the-mill float-fishing anywhere along the river. A hollow glass or carbon fibre match rod fits the bill and will handle most fish, even specimen barbel at a pinch. But for extensive long-trotting for chub down the centre or far side of the middle reaches, something slightly more powerful is called for. A general purpose float rod with a whippy action is ideal for this job. This rod can also be used for casting those heavy swimfeeders as well as light legering.

For more heavy legering, and serious swim-feeder fishing, involving weights of an ounce or more, a purpose-designed leger rod is required. Ten-footers are popular and these can also be used for bream fishing on the lower reaches. Most leger rods are supplied with a screw fitting to take a quiver tip (which is necessary for bream), but a completely separate very flexible top joint called a 'soft top' is often preferred by the matchmen. Those 7ft to 8ft leger rods are not much use on the middle and lower reaches, though they come in handy on the narrow shallow stretches of the upper river. Roach poles, usually 18ft to 21ft in length, are used for bleak fishing and most experts prefer the take-apart rather than the telescopic models. When fly-fishing for trout, grayling, or chub, a 9ft rod with a no 6 line is adequate for most swims. Pike rods need to be on the long side, around 11ft, to cope with reed-beds and precarious banks, while the salmon anglers normally use 9ft spinning rods.

Reels, Lines and Hooks
It is rare to see centre pins on the Severn these days, though in the hands of an expert they enable perfect float control in the steadier swims. A few match anglers still use them occasionally, but open and closed-face fixed spools are the normal equipment—the former for float-fishing fine lines and the latter for long-trotting and legering. While the type of reel is a personal choice, an extra supply of spools carrying varying, breaking strain lines, is a must. These should range from 2lb to $2\frac{1}{2}$lb for general, light float-fishing; 3lb to $3\frac{1}{2}$lb for chubbing and light legering; to 4lb, 5lb or even 6lb for heavy legering and swimfeeder fishing.

Hook-length strengths really depend on how the fish are feeding and the style or method being used. One pound bottoms are quite common among match-anglers when float-fishing and the size of the fish they can land on this frail tackle is surprising. On the other hand, chub and barbel will often accept hooks tied direct to 4lb and 5lb lines. Hook sizes vary enormously and the complete angler carries a range from size 4 to size 20. Size 18 hooks are commonly used for maggots and casters, though when the fish are feeding like mad you ran scale down to a size 14. For legering luncheon meat, breadflake fishing for chub etc, hooks as large as size 4 are not unusual though obviously most anglers begin with something smaller, say a size 10 or 8, scaling down only when they know the fish are taking.

WAGGLER

WAGGLER

Fig 1 Waggler floats: (*above*) waggler with inset; (*below*) straight waggler

By and large, the hook size is a matter of common sense, matching it to the bait and the feeding temperament of the fish.

Floats

Floats for the Severn should be buoyant as plenty of lead shot is needed to cope with the powerful flow. Balsas are probably the most widely used ranging from slim models carrying two BB shot, to huge cigar-shaped patterns which will support up to six swan shot. This may seem a lot of lead but it is necessary to aid casting and float control when trotting big baits at long distances. 'Wagglers' made from peacock quills are popular floats on the middle reaches where they enable small baits to be fished fine and far off in all sorts of conditions. Stick floats come into their own on the steadier lengths where immaculate line control is necessary. Sliding floats are essential on the lower river where the depth is often much greater than the length of the average rod. The top ring of a slider is best placed quite near the tip to aid line control. For the very shallow stretches 'Billy Lane'-type Trent trotters are ideal.

Lead Shot

Swan, AAA and BB shot are an essential part of the Severn angler's tackle box as many swims call for plenty of weight to get the bait down quickly. Smaller shot such as nos 4, 6 and 8, are used near the hook with baits like casters and maggots, especially at hard fished venues where the fish are a bit nervous. Swan shot are also useful for legering on a

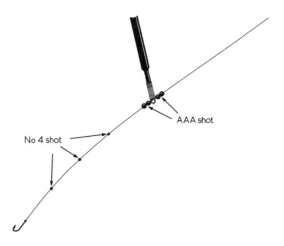

Fig 2 Waggler fishing: the heavy AAA shot are grouped at the base of the float to give casting weight. The lighter No 4 shot are evenly spaced to present a slowly falling bait

sliding link as a string of three or four often holds the bottom better than a single lead of equivalent weight. Arlesey bombs, ranging from $\frac{1}{4}$oz to 1oz are the most widely used leger leads but sometimes the current is so powerful that even a 1oz bomb won't hold the bottom. In these conditions flat leads are a better bet.

General
An important accessory for the Severn is a long, stable rod-rest. This can be a great help for legering and swimfeeder fishing along the middle reaches, when it is important to keep as much line off the water as possible. A rest 4ft to 5ft long, enables the angler to position the rod almost vertically thus achieving the desired effect. Catapults are needed for loose feeding at long range and (if you are not a very good thrower) can also be useful for hurling balls of groundbait.

A large landing-net is a 'must' for lifting big chub and barbel. The modern fibreglass handles which extend from 6ft to 8ft are ideal and allow the fish to be netted well away from the bank. Keep-nets should, of course, comply with

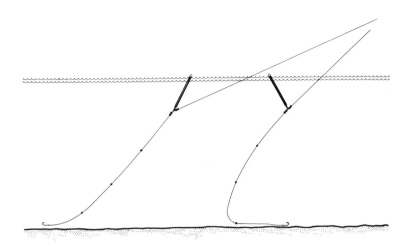

Fig 3 The waggler float in action: it can be checked slightly so that the bait precedes the float through the swim (*left*) or fished over-depth at the speed of the current so that the bait drags on the bottom behind the float as it proceeds through the swim (*right*)

Severn byelaws in length and diameter but, bearing in mind the huge catches that are possible, it pays to obtain a pretty big one. The knotless, micromesh nets, designed specifically for barbel, are the only type worth considering as they are less damaging to all species.

Sliding Float

In swims over 10ft deep, which are the rule rather than the exception on the lower river and which you are also likely to encounter at a few venues on the middle river, it is sometimes awkward to cast a fixed float any great distance. Yet it is often necessary to fish well out when the river is low as the chub make for the middle of the river where the current is faster. The fish also tend to lie in mid-water which means that they take most baits on the drop. While legering is usually the answer to long-casting in deep water it is not very efficient for indicating 'drop bites'—though the experts can detect them. A much better way, providing the wind is favourable, is to use a sliding float. In fact there is no better float for signalling 'lift bites' at long range than a slider. The reason is that a slider, carrying plenty of lead shot, is vertical almost from the moment it hits the surface and it is easier to spot bites in this position than with a conventional fixed float which cocks slowly. For most of the time, until the shot sinks, an ordinary fixed float slants along the surface and it is impossible to distinguish lift bites at any distance, whereas the slider gives almost immediate indication. Nationally famous match-angler Clive Smith has designed a special slider for the lower Severn, mainly for chub fishing, but it also works for other species. The conditions must be right though as it cannot be held in check like a fixed float.

This is how Clive's method works: initially you will see that the first position that the float assumes is after the swan shot have dropped and before the AAA shot has taken effect. At this time it stands high in the water, showing a broad white band. If a fish takes the bait at this stage the float stays high too long, so indicating a bite. But often the fish takes as the AAA shot is reaching the vertical position and has almost pulled the float down. When this happens the float comes up again and the bite is easily distinguished. Sometimes, of course, fish take the bait on the bottom, pulling the float under in the usual manner. In effect, therefore, the slider gives three types of bite indication.

But besides signalling bites, and bearing in mind that chub are the main quarry, the slider has other advantages. Firstly, there is no 'skidding' and disturbance when striking as with normal bulky chub tackle. Secondly, the float offers no resistance on the strike, ensuring that the hook is driven home more positively. Clive makes all his own sliders for this kind of fishing, and on inspection you will notice that they are slightly different to those sold in the shops. The top ring, for instance, is very close to the tip—this is to stop the line sinking which could interfere with control and striking (remember we are fishing a fairly fast stream). The diameter of the top ring is 15 thou, which is small enough to stop a nylon depth-knot. The bottom ring is actually a piece of the top joint of a hollow glass rod which Clive uses because the heavy load of shot damages the more usual wire ring when a hard strike is made. The hollow glass can be any diameter and all he does is to trim a bit from each side of a ¾in piece leaving a strip at each end to whip it to the base of the float. The bottom of the balsa float body is hardened with Araldite, again to prevent damage as the shot flies up on the strike. Most usually, four swan shot and one AAA are used, and nine times out of ten that is the usual loading. To carry this sort of weight the smallest float is about 6in long. Don't forget that a cast of 20yd or more is needed and that we are fishing in from 10ft to 12ft of water.

Loose feeding is impossible in these circumstances so plenty of groundbait is necessary to carry casters or maggots. Care is needed when mixing the groundbait for the consistency should depend on how the fish are feeding. The drill is—quite sloppy if the fish are taking on the drop near the surface, or stiffened in proportion if they are found lower down. Clive's basic shotting doesn't vary very much and he always puts the bulk about four feet from the hook. Sometimes he places an AAA shot on each side of the swan shot to help hold them in place. The bottom AAA is the one varied most and this is positioned according to how the fish are taking. If they are biting well on the drop he lengthens the tail, but if they are on the bottom he sometimes shortens it to five or six inches. Clive's method and technique has been well tried and proven over a number of years, especially in the area between Stourport and Worcester. But it is effective in any deep water swim, close in or far out—providing conditions allow. As I stressed earlier, the float cannot be held in check which, alas, is all too often necessary along the Severn.

Bait

Chub on slices of banana, barbel on bacon rinds and boiled ham, pike on breadflake, roach on sultanas . . . these are some of the unusual baits that have tempted Severn fish over the years. So it is obvious that, as in all fast-flowing rivers, the fish will sample almost anything that passes by, which leaves plenty of leeway for experiment in the bait department. By and large though, the caster is the number one bait for most species all along the Severn.

Maggots, especially bronze-coloured ones, are very much in vogue at the time of writing and it wouldn't surprise me to see this bait oust casters in the popularity stakes in the future. If this should happen, no one will be more mystified as to why than myself. I think that a bait's effectiveness is sometimes merely the result of a kind of psychological vicious circle. Anglers copy each other slavishly and concentrate more on a new 'in' bait to the detriment of the previous one. In other words, if everyone uses bronze-coloured maggots the fish become preoccupied with them and won't look at casters. I am sure this is the only reason why any bait is effective—because it is what the fish come to expect. Nevertheless, I don't think the caster will ever lose its appeal. It is a bait that attracts just about every species, both in summer and winter, and therefore should have a high priority. But no matter what bait is used on the Severn, the most important point is to throw in plenty of feed. Little and often is the drill in normal conditions, as the powerful currents soon wash it away. Having said that I should add that there are times when restraint is necessary, such as when there is cold dam water running through and the fish are finicky. Often at these times the angler who keeps his hand out of the tin enjoys the best sport.

Maggots

Generally speaking, ordinary commercial maggots (the bigger the better) are good enough for the swifter swims on the middle and upper reaches as the fish haven't got time to inspect the bait. As I have already pointed out, bronze-coloured maggots are popular and they can be dyed this shade quite easily with chrysodine powder. On the slower stretches 'gozzers' and 'pinkies' are useful, especially when bream are expected. Squatts are a must on the lower river for attracting bream, and match-anglers think nothing of using half-a-gallon in a five-hour match. This small larvae of the house-fly can also be used on the hook—two or three at a time—when the bream are slow to take. Pinkies also make a good hook bait for roach.

Casters

Casters were first introduced to the Severn around 1963 and since then this bait has accounted for some phenomenal catches. Barbel, chub, roach, dace, in fact anything that swims seems to like them and, as with maggot, the bigger they are the better. Most experts supplement their feed when caster fishing with hempseed and this certainly brings results. In fact, in the summer you can get away with loose feeding hemp and using casters on the hook, and this dodge helps to cut down on expenses.

Tares

Tares made a tremendous impact at many venues during the hot summers of 1975 and 1976, accounting for fantastic hauls of roach approaching the 100lb mark. In conjunction with hempseed feed this 'bean' also attracts barbel and chub and obviously has great possibilities. It is most effective when float-fished but I know several top anglers who catch good bags legering it.

Luncheon Meat

Luncheon meat first became popular as a deadly barbel bait but it is now a top attractor for chub, particularly in the winter months. It is most effective when anchored with a leger but some huge catches have been taken with it on the float. Because of its tendency to fly off the hook when casting or to wash off in strong currents, many anglers prefer a luncheon meat paste which they make up mixing the meat with corn-flour. This can be moulded firmly round the shank of the hook where it stays put in the fastest currents.

Cheese

Cheese, or cheese paste, has lost some of its charm these days, but it is still a wonderful bait for chub and barbel. I wouldn't be a bit surprised to see it come back into prominence in the near future. Used on the leger it often tempts good sample fish when they refuse conventional offerings. The drawback with cheese is its tendency to harden in cold water, but the answer is to use a soft variety such as Edam, or the processed type. Cheese paste is equally as good and this can be easily made with a slice of fresh bread. The late Bill Norry, from Ironbridge, (a famous Severn-wise angler), was a great believer in cheese paste and he liked it really 'smelly'. He confessed to keeping it in airtight bags for weeks at a time to allow it to mature.

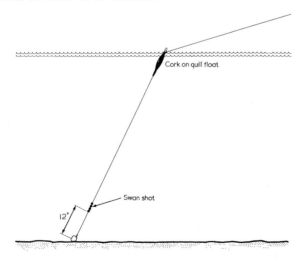

Fig 4 A typical rig for breadflake fishing. The float is sufficiently buoyant to support a bunch of swan shot placed 12in from the baited hook

31

One of the deadliest of all Severn chub baits is the wasp grub. Nests like this one provide the angler with both white grubs for hookbait and mashed up cake for groundbait.

Breadflake
Breadflake is a top chub bait in clear conditions and also excellent for bream on the lower reaches. Ordinary freshly sliced loaves (being moist) are ideal as the flake really clings to the hook. A piece the size of a 50p piece squeezed onto the shank of a size 10 or 8 hook and trotted down the middle is often irresistible to big chub. But, of course, for bream it has to be legered.

Wasp Grub
Wasp grub is a great summer bait for chub, so good in fact that it has been banned in most association and open matches on the premise that it is unfair to competitors without a supply. Nevertheless there is nothing to prevent anyone using it on a pleasure outing, so full details on finding, preparing and using this bait are covered in another chapter.

Stewed Wheat

Stewed wheat has its moments on the Severn in summer and autumn and attracts top-quality roach and chub as well as dace. Cheap, clean and easy to prepare, it is a bait that in my opinion has never really been fully exploited, though on the other hand a few old-timers swear by it.

Worms

Worms, both lobs and small reds, are useful for barbel and chub, trout and eels, particularly when there is 'a drop on'. A point to make here is that almost without exception all the double figure barbel taken from the Severn have fallen for a bunch of lobworms. I am certain that many more big barbel would be landed if more anglers used this bait in quantity as did the old Trent fishermen. They ladled in thousands of lobworms before a barbel session and their results were phenomenal.

Groundbait

Cereal groundbait, other than for bream, has gone out of fashion on the Severn, most anglers preferring to loose feed their swims. Nevertheless it is useful sometimes in very fast water to help get the hook bait samples quickly on the bottom. Medium breadcrumb is the most widely used, but the important thing is to mix it really thoroughly otherwise it will float in the river's powerful currents. The best way is to wet an initial quantity so that it is really soggy and then gradually add dry crumbs until it is the right consistency. On the lower river groundbait is vital and large quantities are needed to attract the bream. Again, medium breadcrumb is used but it should be mixed really heavy so that it sinks like a stone. Some anglers add a little silver sand or maize meal to help it sink quickly but there is no need for this if the breadcrumb is really well soaked. The dodge here is to take your time mixing it, allowing the crumbs to absorb plenty of water.

Part 3
Match Fishing

A Tough Test

As a match river the Severn is a tough testing ground, and though the rewards both in sport and big cash prizes can be high, it has a reputation as a heartbreaker and a deflater of egos. To master both the middle and lower reaches (few events take place on the upper river) in all its moods demands a proficiency in most fishing methods and techniques that few anglers ever attain. Those that do, however, often become leaders in this branch of the sport as the skills they learn on the Severn hold them in good stead on most other waters. The top Severn match-anglers are experts at legering for bream, trotting the stream for chub and roach, 'barbel bashing' with a swimfeeder as well as 'snatching' dace and bleak. And, perhaps more important, they know just when and where to use the right method.

This question of tactics is always a difficult problem on the Severn, much more so than on other match rivers, which is why experts from other areas often come unstuck. For example, bleak win many matches along the lower reaches, but fishing for them can be a complete waste of time in certain circumstances, for instance if the bream or chub happen to be moving well. I have watched bleak specialists work like automatons for five hours to whip out a creditable teens of pounds haul only to find themselves well down the prize list because the bream have been feeding. Similar problems arise along the middle reaches and when faced with a bewildering choice between float, leger or swimfeeder, fishing close in or far out, with a variety of baits that could all catch, even the experts sometimes make a wrong decision.

The luck of the draw is also very important as many venues are extremely patchy and this is why big matches are sometimes won by inexperienced anglers, especially in the summer when barbel seem to give themselves up to anyone using a swimfeeder. But the men who regularly make the frame are invariably dedicated enthusiasts who spend as much time as possible fishing and talking about the Severn. This is the only way to learn its mysteries. Unlike, say the Trent, Witham, or Welland, there are no hard-and-fast-rules to follow—adaptability is the key to success. As an example of the problems involved consider the choice of match baits. Until the summer of 1975 this was reasonably straight-forward in as much as casters were tops at most venues. But no longer can they be relied on to bring a winning catch. Bronze-coloured maggots are now very much in vogue, as are tares in summer. Luncheon meat is always a potential match winner so that cannot be ruled out. Neither can bread-flake or wasp grub if it is allowed. All in all, the match-angler needs a lot of experience plus a great deal of confidence to be able to make the right choice.

Perhaps I can give a clearer picture of what is involved in Severn match fishing by describing the methods and tactics used at summer contests on the river between Stourport and Worcester, an area where float and leger techniques still hold their own against the swimfeeder.

Methods and Tactics

The well-equipped entrant normally carries around four pints of casters, two or three pints of maggots, a good supply of tares and plenty of hempseed. The latter is used in the feed for all species, no matter what is put on the hook. 'Save' baits such as breadflake and luncheon meat are also packed into the basket. If the river is low and clear and there is plenty of room to work some experts always begin operations by trotting breadflake or, again if it is allowed, wasp grub down the middle for chub. But the large majority usually plump for casters offered well out with a 'waggler' float, a method that will catch any species. But, at the same time, they feed tares or maggots ready for a switch if their first choice is unsuccessful.

The waggler method is by far the most popular in the shallower stretches as it enables lightly shotted terminal tackle to be cast over long distances and also allows for more control in windy conditions. The float is locked in place with the bulk shot and a few no 4s are fastened at intervals towards the hook. If the bait is being dragged well on the bottom, dust shot are sometimes squeezed on the hook length to help slow the bait's travel. Although good-sized chub or barbel are expected, line strength and hook lengths are kept as fine as possible. Two-and-a-half-pound reel line with one-and-a-half pound hook bottoms are quite usual. Hooks are normally on the small side—size 18 is a popular choice, though a change to something larger fastened to stronger line is made if big fish come regularly. These light rigs, of course, attract fish at all depths and therefore offer the most chances of getting bites which after all is what it's all about.

Feeding the swim is of prime importance, and while the

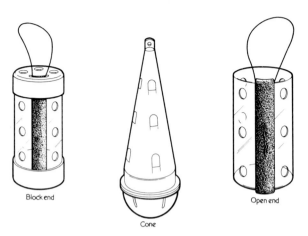

Block end

Cone

Open end

Fig 5 Three popular types of swimfeeder commonly used on the Severn

float is being carefully manipulated down the chosen line, loose feed (groundbait is rarely used) is constantly catapulted to the head of the swim—at least once every cast, and sometimes more. Many experts cast out, drop the rod in a rest, catapult the feed and pick up the rod again before the float has settled. If barbel are in evidence, stouter tackle —3lb line and $2\frac{1}{2}$lb bottoms—and maybe a different method such as a swimfeeder must be considered. This gadget has made a tremendous impact on Severn match fishing and is mainly responsible for the ever spiralling weights of recent years. Top names, who achieved their reputations with the float on the upper reaches or with the leger on the lower river, naturally resent this seemingly easy method of building up a big weight.

But is it always that simple? There is much more to successful 'feeder' fishing than appears on the surface, otherwise why do certain specialists do so well? Mind you, sticking religiously to this method has its draw-backs and sometimes the 'feeder men' are left at the post. This was brought home to me at one of the popular Stourport Opens when I saw a prominent swimfeeder expert struggling for bites on one of the best roach pegs along the stretch

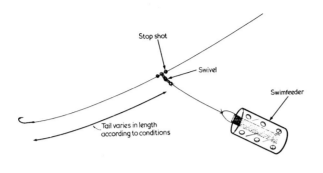

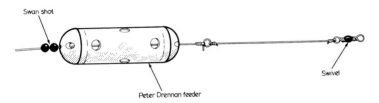

Fig 6 Typical swimfeeder rigs. Both are fished on paternoster links attached to the main line by a swivel and prevented from sliding by stop shot

and on a day when the roach were going mad. While the float anglers were hauling in fish after fish, our friend caught so little he never bothered to weigh in. On the other hand I watched the same angler at a Worcester Open net double-figures of small fish off an unrated peg to finish high in the prize list. Confidence in the gadget I would put as the main reason for the success of the feeder experts. That and their willingness to spend a small fortune on maggots and casters. They get through enormous quantities in summer using anything up to 12 pints in a five-hour contest.

But to get back to the match—if the barbel are close in, the float can hold its own with the feeder as Bewdley angler Graham Parker demonstrated at the 1976 Birmingham AA Team Championships. Drawn at Hampton Loade, on the left bank near the bottom of the spinney, Graham began the match with a swimfeeder but when he realised he was sitting

41

almost on top of a huge shoal of barbel he changed to a stick float and hammered out 80lb in four hours for a great individual win. Stick floats and slim balsas are widely used in the steadier swims for dace and roach, and if the roach do turn up this is definitely the float that catches them with tares. On some days it is possible to get the roach feeding immediately on this comparatively new Severn bait, but most entries make the switch gradually and feed tares while offering the more traditional loose feed at first. Presented singly on a size 16 or 14 hook, tares attract a better stamp of fish—chub and barbel as well as roach. When float tactics fail, a change to legering or a feeder, in order to offer a still bait, is the normal practice. If large quantities of casters or maggots have been chucked in the swim it's as well to stick to these on the hook for a further try before changing to something completely different such as luncheon meat.

Not that meat is merely a last resort bait. On the contrary, many star matchmen will have concentrated with this bait from the off, either legered or with a swimfeeder, but it is normally only a winner when the river is below par. These general middle river tactics are applicable at all venues above and below Stourport providing the depth allows. But downstream from Worcester, bream begin to figure in catches, particularly in the deeper stretches and on these lengths the approach is quite different. Legering now becomes a first choice method for the majority of entries, and for this a 9ft or 10ft rod with a quiver tip or soft top is essential as the bites are often delicate. The most common terminal rig is the paternoster with an Arlesey bomb ranging between $\frac{1}{2}$oz and 1oz. This is fastened to a sliding link with a small swivel stopped 2ft or 3ft from the hook.

Bream normally lie tightly shoaled in the deeper holes, so the first few casts are more or less exploratory to find the deepest part of the swim and to ensure that the bottom is clean—there are many snaggy pitches on the lower river. Once a mark has been decided upon the next step is to lay a thick carpet of groundbait in an area about 9ft square. Ten minutes spent doing this at the start of a match is time well spent, as it is often fatal to throw groundbait in once the bream are feeding. If more should be necessary, it is best to wait until a boat passes as the fish are accustomed to this sort of surface disturbance and will not notice the splash of a ball of groundbait. The hook bait for bream is usually a straight choice between 'gozzers' or breadflake. If maggots are preferred, and they do have the advantage of being less selective, squatts or pinkies are added to the groundbait. A few casters always help to attract bream though they are not so good on the hook which, incidentally, is either a size 16, 18, or 20 depending on how the bream are taking. For breadflake, a size 10 is more suitable for the usual 5p-sized offering.

Bream are by no means spread evenly along the lower river, however; there are many deep stretches where chub are more likely to be in residence. This is when the sliding float technique comes in useful. A good sized balsa model carrying at least three swan shot is necessary to cope with the powerful flow and this should be stopped so that the bait just bounces along the bottom. Because chub often take in mid-water the shot should be carefully placed so that 'drop bites' are instantly signalled (this method is explained fully elsewhere). Baits for chub are the same as the middle reaches, but loose feeding is out of the question and plenty of groundbait is required. The roach in the lower river can be caught close in where the depth averages between 8ft and 12ft and in these swims normal float tactics are suitable. Bleak are prolific almost everywhere below Worcester, but going all out for them is always a gamble in a big match. Most top names seek the bream, chub or roach at first and only switch to 'bleaking' as a last resort. Nevertheless the tiny blighters often form the bulk of winning weights, so it pays to do plenty of homework before a contest in order to find out whether they will figure.

The biggest match held on the river, and one that all Midland match-anglers aspire to win, is the mammoth Birmingham Anglers' Association Annual which takes place traditionally on the first Sunday in October. This popular contest (which is also spread along the River Avon) attracts 4,000 entries, most of whom hope to draw a peg on the middle reaches of the Severn. But many are disappointed as the pegs are staked out along the BAA stretches and those loaned by clubs and associations on both banks of the river between Tewkesbury and Shrewsbury. The lucky winner picks up a cash prize of approximately £750 plus a huge trophy. The Birmingham Anglers' Association Welfare contests are also popular, especially those held at Quatford. The two summer matches take place alternately on the lower and middle reaches on the last Sunday in July and the first Sunday in August.

Other main matches through the season (the dates sometimes vary) are: The Worcester Carnival at Worcester on the last Sunday in June; the Bridgnorth Open at Linley on the second Saturday in August (but this may be discontinued); the Severn Championship is on the lower river from Worcester to Tewkesbury on the third Saturday in August; and the BAA Team Championships are at Quatford on the third Sunday in August. The Worcester Orphanage Open takes place at Worcester on the last Sunday in August; and another BAA Welfare, the Alder Cup, is held on the third Sunday in November. On the second Sunday in December the BAA runs its Joe Miller Christmas contest; and the last big event is the Association's February Welfare on the first Sunday. These matches cater for over 200 entries but there are scores of smaller opens in mid-week and at weekends organised by clubs and associations. These are advertised in the angling press and take place at such venues as Haw Bridge, organised by the Gloucester United and District AA, Tewkesbury (Tewkesbury Popular AA), Kempsey (Kempsey AA), Worcester (Worcester DUAA), Winnals and Bewdley (Kidderminster DAA) Holt Fleet (through various clubs and individuals), Ironbridge (various clubs) and Shrewsbury (various clubs).

Part 4
The Fish

Barbel

The middle reaches of the Severn must be the most prolific barbel water in the country bar none. Yet, incredibly, the species were non-existent in the river before 1956. In that year what can only be regarded as the most significant decision ever to influence angling was made when the old Severn River Authority was persuaded by *The Angling Times* to introduce the species. Five-hundred-and-nine barbel, ranging up to 9lb in weight, were taken from the River Kennet, in Berkshire, and placed in the Severn at nine different points between Shrewsbury and Bewdley. Little was heard of these fish for the next ten years, indeed they were almost forgotten. But towards the end of the 1960s, more and more reports of barbel catches began to hit the headlines and it became apparent that they were well-established. By the early 1970s, barbel had become the dominant species in some areas. In fact they bred so fast that there were fears that other species were being pushed out of their traditional haunts.

Fortunately what became known as the barbel 'explosion' seems to have subsided a little and with roach, chub and dace returning in fair numbers, a balance between the different species is taking place. Nevertheless, barbel are still the dominant fish in many stretches of the river, and no doubt will continue to be so for many years to come. It is interesting to note that the barbel have stayed more or less near the original dropping points such as Atcham, Coalport, Hampton Loade and Bewdley though, inevitably, large shoals have become established elsewhere. Some have surmounted the weir at Shrewsbury and made their way upstream as far as the Vyrnwy and Camlad tributaries, and many barbel are now settled as far downstream as Tewkesbury.

Generally speaking, Severn barbel are on the small side,

no doubt because there are so many of them, but shoals of 5lb and 6lb fish are becoming more prevalent. Plenty of barbel around the 7lb mark were taken in 1978, a season incidentally that saw fewer small fish landed, so perhaps we can expect even bigger specimens in the near future.

There *are* good barbel in the river, that's for sure, but finding them and catching them is no easy task. To my knowledge less than a dozen double-figure fish have been landed, and three of these were taken out of season by salmon anglers. Severn-Trent Authority netsmen have reported seeing fish up to 14lb while carrying out electro-netting operations, and there are countless stories of monsters hooked and lost. Almost without exception these big fish have been seen or hooked in areas where there are fewer small barbel.

The biggest authenticated barbel (in as much as it was weighed and photographed) was an eleven-pounder landed by young Harold Lawton from the town water at Ironbridge.

Dennis Boden cradles an 8lb barbel, one of the many specimens taken each year from the river

The pitch where he concentrates most of his efforts is on the Dawley AC day-ticket stretch of the right bank, on a point above a large bay, and he offers his baits at the edge of the stream beyond the backwater in a swim 12ft deep.

The Leighton Salmon and Coarse Fishing Club water, a few miles upstream, produces plenty of barbel between six and eight pounds and it was here that a twelve-and-a-half-pounder was taken on a bunch of lobworms by a salmon angler. Still further upstream, at Cound Lodge on the BAA water, shoals of barbel up to 8lb, occasionally up to 9lb, turn up now and then. This is the venue where Wolverhampton angler Ron Baker landed a super twenty-fish haul of barbel of between 5lb and 8lb apiece from a pitch at the back of the pub. The bottom end of the Severn-Trent Water Authority stretch at Atcham is another better-class barbel water. Plenty of fish up to 8lb are hooked in this area, especially on the long straight length below the confluence of the Tern. The 'hot spot' here is a swim pin-pointed by two stumps sticking up out of the water. Weir pools have always been noted as big barbel haunts on many rivers but for some reason they do not attract the Severn species. At least, few are taken from the pool at Shrewsbury though a twelve-and-a-half-pounder was landed (again out of season by a salmon angler) 300yd downstream of the weir.

Of the bigger-barbel haunts I have mentioned, the only common factor is, as I said earlier, that they are in areas where there are few shoals of small fish. Below Stourport, for instance, barbel are very thinly spread but the few known 'hot spots' produce better-class fish. Five-pounders are a good average at some venues notably the top of the Birmingham AA's Grimley stretch and the 'cables' area on Worcester DUAA's Beauchamp Court length. And this could be the clue to locating specimens as it is rare to find mixed-size shoals. Anglers seeking better-class barbel should steer clear of the more popular venues. Severn barbel are almost predictable in their habits, at any rate this applies to medium and small-sized fish, and their fondness for shoaling tightly in the same swim year after year makes them an easy target.

But why they prefer one area to another in more or less identical stretches of the river is something of a mystery. For this reason it is often a waste of time searching for likely swims. I could take you to what appear to be perfect barbel haunts—that is smooth-flowing glides running swiftly over a gravel or slab-rocked bottom—in areas known to hold the species and you would more than likely draw a blank or at best catch only a couple. Yet move a few yards downstream or upstream to an insignificant-looking swim and your bait might well be taken each time it hits bottom.

Generally, barbel tend to congregate at the head or tail of fords or in the deeper pools which invariably follow. Sometimes they are present in very turbulent water, providing there is some kind of shelter such as a channel or a few boulders where they can rest from the force of the current. On the other hand they are not averse to deep, steady or slack water on the edge of eddies or bays, as anyone who has fished the well known barbel swims at the top of the BAA Danery stretch will verify. That barbel prefer a nice clean bottom is fairly common knowledge and most of the better-known Severn pitches fit this description.

I suppose, that all things considered, the basic drawing factor boils down to the food supply trickling into or already present in a swim. In other words, they collect in places where they can obtain most food. An interesting point about barbel swims, and one that can be very useful to know, is that there is nearly always a 'hot spot' somewhere among the shoal where the fish lie almost on top of each other. A theory put forward to explain these 'hot spots' is that because the areas to which the current carries the food are limited, as many fish as possible gather there to feed until they are replete and then move out to be immediately replaced by others in the shoal. Barbel feed freely at all times of the day and are not, like many other species, put off by bright sunlight or bankside activity. Evening is probably the most rewarding time and certainly the better-class fish are taken as darkness is falling. And, if night fishing were allowed on some stretches, I dare say more of the monsters known to be in the river would be tempted to take the bait. One thing barbel cannot stand is a drop in the water temperature—a fall of one degree is often enough to put them down or off feeding, which is unfortunate as the Severn suffers from frequent discharges of cold dam water. Although this 'compensation water', as it is called, has little effect on sport during the very hot weather, it is often enough to kill sport completely in cooler conditions. On the other hand a rise in the river level due to extra rainfall will frequently set them off feeding like mad. The barbel is well equipped to withstand the extra water and they appear to stay in their regular haunts no matter how high the river rises. This is important to remember as most of us tend to seek steadier water close in at such times.

Come the first frosts of autumn and you can almost forget Severn barbel. True, odd fish are caught regularly all through the colder months. True also that a few reasonable bags are landed during the milder spells when the river has lifted slightly. But generally the species seem to go into semi-hibernation, lying stationary on the river bed and eating very little if anything at all. In many parts of the river the shoals stay in their summer haunts and make little effort to seek deeper and warmer holes. Indeed they have not much choice in this respect unless they travel many miles, and this they are reluctant to do after October according to findings made with tagged fish.

However, if there is a deep hole anywhere in the vicinity barbel will move into it and perhaps because they are more comfortable can be persuaded to feed. At Cound Lodge, near Cressage, for instance, there is a deep salmon pool immediately above a popular shallow barbel swim and there is no doubt that is where they go in the winter. Several reputable catches over the years have proved this. The bottom end of the BAA stretch at Quatford is another area where deeper water, surrounded by shallows, becomes more popular in winter. Well-known match angler Geoff Morris, from Halesowen, can verify this as he once caught an incredible 40lb of barbel in a contest late in November 1975,

51

from just above the island. This particular pitch rarely shines in the summer—the adjacent shallow water is far more rewarding—but the barbel were there in huge quantities on that bitterly cold Sunday.

In contrast another impressive winter catch came from a shallow length just below Tern mouth at Atcham, near Shrewsbury, in the middle of January. The river was starting to rise that day, and in a torrential downpour Wolverhampton angler Ron Baker landed half-a-dozen barbel all around the 6lb mark. I should add that the winter that year was quite mild, which perhaps explains why several outstanding catches were made at widely separated venues both in the preceding and following weeks of Baker's haul. The key to the problem of catching barbel in winter is the temperature of the river.

Barbel just don't like cold water, it is as simple as that. If a fall in temperature of one or two degrees is enough to put them off feed in summer, it is little wonder that few are caught in winter. But find a spot where the water is slightly warmer, or wait for a mild spell or a spate and there is a chance, albeit a small one, of tempting a few fish. Of course, even on cold days, if you can drop the bait in their mouths as it were, they will probably take it if only by instinct rather than inclination. This is, I feel, the explanation for all those barbel which are hooked when conditions are against us.

I have already stated that barbel lie stationary on the bottom, but what is more interesting is the way they crowd very close together in as small an area as possible. Groups of as many as 100 fish have been observed packed nose-to-tail like interlocked fingers in a space no larger than a dustbin lid. Why they bunch together like this is anybody's guess, but it is my belief that they are attracted by the comparatively warmer water of a spring in the river-bed. Imagine the effect of a bait dropped among such a shoal. One fish would surely grab it, which would suggest that if a barbel is hooked it would be worthwhile to keep casting in exactly the same spot.

Because we need to search for barbel in winter the best method is one that allows the bait to cover as large an area of the river as possible. While float-fishing would perhaps do the job most effectively, there is a snag and that is the fact that the bait also needs to be presented as still as possible —barbel certainly won't chase it. As a float can only be kept in check at close range, a light leger or swimfeeder is the better bet. Then the bait can be rolled slowly in an arc (provided the bottom is snag-free) until the whole swim has been explored. If a barbel is hooked, the exact spot should be noted as the chances are this is where the rest of the shoal are lying.

Winter baits are more or less the same as summer but it pays to use smaller hooks and far less feed. Most Severn experts keep any loose feed to a minimum and often scale down to size 18 hooks tied to $1\frac{1}{2}$lb line. The best method to catch Severn barbel is, without any doubt, the swimfeeder. Despite the controversy that surrounds the gadget (it has been blamed for lowering angling skills, and littering the river bed with smashed tackle) it could have been invented for barbel fishing. In fact, since the feeder became popular in the early 1970s individual and match catches of barbel and other species have spiralled to amazing heights. I have witnessed several in excess of 100lb and can well believe the tales of anglers who have caught so many fish they couldn't lift their nets from the water. Possibly the biggest haul made with a feeder on the river was an estimated 200lb landed by Birmingham angler Ken Henderson from that famous swim 'Harris's Pitch' at Quatford. Ken has netted many big catches from this particular spot and knows it like the back of his hand. But on that memorable day in 1975 everything went like clockwork, and Ken's usual large offerings of maggots (he fed a gallon-and-a-half) provoked the fish into almost fighting to take his bait.

One of the advantages of the feeder is its effectiveness in all types of swims. Fast-flowing rapids, smooth-running glides, deep holes, difficult backswims, snaggy-bottomed gullies, can all be mastered with 'the plastic pig'. Of course, feeder fishing isn't everyone's cup of tea, hence the controversy. And though I sympathise with those highly skilled match-anglers who complain that the feeder puts the most raw novice immediately on a par with top stars, it should be made clear that there is more to the method than simply lobbing out a feeder and sitting back waiting for barbel to hook themselves. Feeder fishing has its own skills as specialists like Geoff Morris, Fred Bailey, Ron Russell and Dennis Boden have proved time and again.

Fred Bailey, who is something of a legend in his own lifetime following years of wonderful catches of most species with widely differing methods, successfully switched to the feeder and now rarely uses any other method. His results with very stout tackle are exceptional by any standards and have done much to persuade other anglers to have a go. Where the feeder scores over other methods for tightly-shoaled barbel is that the hook is always surrounded by samples of the bait no matter how powerful the current. It also keeps the barbel firmly on the bottom where they take the bait more positively.

There are several different models on the market, all made from plastic or perspex, drilled with holes to release the bait and in all manner of sizes. The early versions included a strip of lead attached to one side to act as an anchor, but modern feeders are more streamlined and often incorporate a special compartment which can be loaded with lead shot to suit varying situations. Block-end feeders, that is those with a cap at each end, are best for maggots and sometimes casters, while for other baits the open-ended types are more suitable. These are filled with samples of bait and sealed with ground-bait mixed to suit the strength of the current. Most feeders are cylindrical but the cone-shaped patterns are supposed to help reduce tackle resistance both in the flow and on the strike. This model also cuts down the surface disturbance as it is reeled in. Not that this is particularly important for barbel. In fact it takes a lot to disturb a feeding shoal. Some anglers contend that the splashing of the feeder actually attracts them and they come to associate it with food.

The size of the feeder for barbel is not critical as the fish are not particularly tackle-shy. It should really be governed by the type of swim and the bait being employed—the larger the feeder the more difficult it is to hold the bottom in midstream. On the other hand, there is plenty of evidence that with maggots as bait, the more you put in the more fish come to the hook. Which would suggest a large feeder for maggot bait, that is if your pocket will run to it. Rods for feeder fishing obviously need to be powerful enough to cast the loaded feeder with a high degree of accuracy, but it is important also that it has a flexible tip, both to indicate bites and to cushion the extreme line shock on the strike. An ordinary general purpose 10ft or 11ft leger rod with a special tip is favoured by most experts. Lines are normally around the 3lb to 5lb breaking strain mark which is strong enough to land most Severn fish, but Fred Bailey gets away with an 8lb line used with an ordinary 9ft salmon spinning rod.

How the feeder is attached to the line and the distance between it and the hook depends on the type of swim and general conditions. For instance, turbulent 'boiling' water tends to scatter bait all over the place, and in this situation the feeder would be set perhaps only a foot from the hook. But in low, clear water it is sometimes necessary to increase the distance considerably. Most feeders incorporate a swivel, or loop of nylon, through which the reel line may be threaded; but a better plan is to attach it by a short link—paternoster style. This will help lessen tackle resistance as the barbel takes the bait and also help reduce smashes on the strike. The link can also be used to carry swan shot to help hold the bottom.

One of the main essentials of successful swimfeeder fishing is accurate casting. It is critical that the feeder should land in the same spot every time, or very near, otherwise you will bait up too wide an area. For example, if you cast out and allow the feeder to roll with the current, most of the bait will have been washed out before it comes to rest. Therefore it pays to make a few experimental casts with an empty feeder to size up the speed of the current and the spot where it will most likely stay on the bottom. Having selected a target area, stick with it for a lengthy period and, after a

short while, you will have laid an attractive carpet of bait. Of course, if the bites are not forthcoming or if other, unwanted, species move in, you will have to start searching. Barbel shoals do wander around in summer but the fish may just not be in a feeding mood, in which case a change of bait, or a smaller hook, will be required to tempt an odd fish or two. Feeder bites are generally quite positive but don't make the mistake of always waiting for the rod tip to swing round. Strike at any unusual movement of the line or tip that isn't caused by flow. Only experience can teach you to tell the difference, and this is the big secret behind all those mammoth hauls.

Most anglers experience a lot of missed bites for no apparent reason when feeder fishing. This is sometimes the result of the barbel nudging or picking up the feeder instead of the hook bait, and the answer is to either increase the length of the paternoster link or the distance between the feeder and the hook. Or you could try one of the new camouflaged feeders that are stained black or green. While swimfeeders are normally associated with Severn barbel they also account for good bags of other species. Indeed, the top experts have become so proficient with the method that they catch fast-biting roach and dace, as well as chub. The gadget has also proved its worth for bream on the deep, powerful lower reaches of the river—always a difficult water to master with other methods.

No matter what the critics say, the feeder catches fish, often in difficult conditions, and sooner or later they are bound to accept it as a perfectly good method, with its own skills, that is ideal for the Severn. Former Severn champion Ron Russell firmly believes this. An expert float-angler, Ron had no qualms about switching to the feeder. This is what he has to say on the subject:

(*opposite*) Severn regular, Fred Wilkes, with a 60lb catch of barbel taken from the river at Bewdley

I don't know who first thought up the idea of the swimfeeder, but whoever it was deserves a place in angling history on a par with the inventor of the fixed spool reel for helping the average angler catch fish more easily. The device is so efficient it has virtually taken over the River Severn. So much so that it is rare to see individual anglers float-fishing or legering. And I suspect that many newcomers know no other method. While this is a pity in that they are missing out on the fun and satisfaction gained from traditional Severn methods, it's no good anyone moaning about it. We must accept the fact that the feeder catches fish very easily in the summer and is here to stay. I'm sure that at the moment the technique is still in its infancy and we still have a lot to learn. As the years go by the method will be developed to the extent that the feeder will become like the fixed spool reel—a standard piece of tackle for all waters. The big secret behind successful feeder fishing and those huge catches on the Severn (and this is where most anglers go wrong) is dropping the feeder in the same spot time after time, and even more important, holding it there.

Then you become an instant star groundbaiter as your hook-bait is always surrounded by plenty of feed. While accurate casting is essential to achieve this ideal situation, it is also essential to weight or load the feeder with sufficient lead to make it stay put. The strip of lead fastened to commercial models is nowhere near heavy enough to hold bottom in most areas of the Severn, so I insert a leger lead. A $\frac{3}{4}$ inch coffin-type fits snugly in the bottom of the large block-end feeders and is usually heavy enough to keep it stationary providing there isn't too much pressure on the reel line. And here's another secret. When you cast the feeder—sideways is always best for accuracy, —hold the rod high and lower it with the bail arm open to follow the feeder to the bottom. When you feel the bump, engage the bail arm—not before. If you knock the bail arm on as the feeder hits the water, as many anglers do, you finish up with too much line below the surface. Pressure then builds up and drags the feeder off the target. This is even more pronounced with stout tackle and, as I often use 8lb reel line with a 5lb hook length, it's a point I have to watch all the time. Tackle of such strength may seem unduly powerful but I find it necessary to withstand the strain of casting heavy feeders quite long distances and hauling in the strong barbel through fast currents. The same applies to hooks. I can usually get away with a forged size 12 carrying three maggots (I'm not fond of casters for the hook as they are shelled too easily) so I can't see any point in going smaller unless the fish are not feeding freely.

Then, as with all other methods, is the time to start experimenting. The main drawback in feeder fishing is the amount of bait required to fill it at every cast. It is easy to get through half-a-gallon of maggots or casters in a five-hour session. But you can cut costs when pleasure fishing by adapting the feeder to dispense various groundbait mixtures. One way is to enlarge the holes in a block-end feeder to twice the diameter and fill it with a mix of one pint of maggots to 6 pints of medium breadcrumb groundbait. Don't pack it too tightly, leave room for the maggots to wriggle about so that the groundbait breaks up and trickles through the king-sized holes. Another way is to discard the top cap and wire or nylon loop and fit a large Arlesley bomb through the centre hole in the bottom cap with the swivel protruding. The reel line is then passed through the swivel eye and the feeder hangs open-ended upside down. Fill the feeder with left-over bait—old maggots, casters, luncheon meat, in fact anything you like if you are seeking chub or barbel—and cap it with stiff groundbait. When it hits bottom a short sharp lift of the rod will release the groundbait and spill the attractors all around the hookbait. A snag with a heavy feeder, both when casting and striking, is preventing it sliding down to the hook. Shots alone are ineffective so what I do is tie a four-turn water knot above the hook length and rest a couple of big shot just above the knot. Again let me emphasise that for barbel, and chub, you can fill the feeder with any old rubbish. They are scavenger fish that will eat almost anything.

Bleak

Bleak are abundant in the lower reaches of the river, and though most individual anglers regard them as bait-stealing pests they play an important part in summer matches. Voracious as they are and seemingly always feeding, the Severn variety are nevertheless invariably small and rarely exceed an ounce in weight. However, the expert 'bleak snatchers' think nothing of landing up to 20lb in a five-hour match. This style of angling is not everyone's cup of tea as such a bag would consist of around 600 fish, which works out at 120 an hour, or 2 per minute—a machine-like operation. In fact, a notable top 'bleaker', international match-angler Bob Tromans from Tipton, West Midlands, reckons he feels and acts like a machine once he has got into his stride. This is what Bob has to say about his 'bleaking' methods:

The basic tool for bleak snatching is a light roach pole used without a reel and with the line tied direct to the tip. If you want to catch several fish a minute the rod needs to become an extension of the arm—you don't want to even think about it. Certainly a reel has no part to play. I use a telescopic, hollow fibreglass pole, usually in a 14ft length. It is very light but firm and stiff, and the handle (I have discarded the thick butt piece except for emergencies when the bleak won't come close in) is slim enough for me to hold comfortably for very long periods. The top joint is the only part I have found necessary to alter. The original tip was too stiff for my liking so I chopped 18in off and spliced on an 18in length of solid fibreglass which I filed and tapered down to about a one-sixteenth of an inch diameter tip. Finally I whipped on a small loop of 18lb breaking strain nylon which I use for fastening on my main line. I find that this flexible tip enables me to handle any sizeable fish which take the bait intended for bleak. Although I use a float when bleaking, its purpose is not for indicating bites. I am usually lifting the fish from the water before any movement has registered on the float. I know this puzzles many anglers for I have heard them talking while they have been watching me fish. Some of the explanations they dream up as to how I know there is a bleak on are fantastic, yet the answer is simple —I watch the hook maggot. I keep my eyes glued to it as it slowly sinks, suddenly it disappears as a bleak takes it and I lift the fish out straifght to my hand. I would be too late most times if I waited for the float to signal a bite, for bleak are very fast and can suck a maggot dry and spit it out while you are blinking an eye. When the river is normal it is possible to watch the maggot sink quite a depth, but I rarely let it go above a foot before I re-cast and try again. Of course, when the river is coloured after a spate, it is not possible to see the maggot. I then watch the line itself for my bite indication. It is surprising how well the line shows up on rippled water and it is easy to see it shoot along the surface as a bleak takes the maggot. To make it even more outstanding, I often smear vaseline along the hook length and on the loops where it joins the main line. These loops, when well greased, make a great bite indicator which stands out a mile, showing up the slightest movement of the hook length below. When I see the slight pull on the line signifying a bite up goes my arm and the bleak swings straight

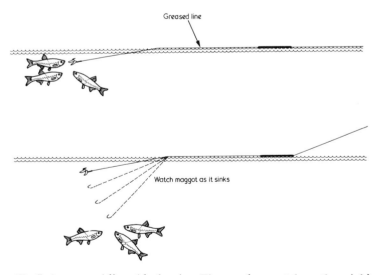

Fig 7 A greased-line bleak rig. The angler watches the sinking maggot, not the float, for indications of a bite

out. I don't strike, it's not necessary. The bleak is soft-mouthed and the mere lifting of the pole and consequently the line, at the same time as the bleak is taking the maggot, is enough to set the hook. When I lift the fish and swing it in I keep my right arm slightly extended and then I know that the bleak will come straight to my left hand. I measure out my main line for just this purpose. The length is approximately 13ft, a foot less than my pole, then with a 2ft hook length the whole line allows me to bring the fish to hand quite comfortably. I carry a few longer lengths made up to 17ft for the odd occasion when I use the 18ft pole. All my lines are made up with a loop at each end from 2½lb breaking strain nylon, and I keep them on cork wrappers. The floats I use are small two-inch plastic 'duckers' made, I think, by the firm which makes those artificial baits. I find they are ideal for 'bleaking', at least for the purpose I use them, which is to provide just enough weight for a controlled cast and yet not too much to offer resistance when a bleak pulls the bait. I always tie the float to the line 4ft from the hook.

It is a fixed knot and once it is tied I cannot move the float one way or the other. Not that I ever want to for it is there only, as I said earlier, to aid my casting. The reason I tie it 4ft from the hook is because I have found that it is the best position to allow me to drop my line on the water in a wavy line and not straight—important this for it reduces resistance as the bleak 'takes'. So far, apart from my floats, my tackle has not differed greatly from most other Midland 'bleakers'. It's when we start talking about hook sizes that my ideas differ. The fact is I prefer the smaller sizes tied to fine nylon. An 18 is my favourite and I use this whenever possible tied to 1½lb or sometimes 1lb line. I never go larger than a 16 or smaller than a 20. Compared with the traditional size 14 tied to 2½lb nylon my hook tackles are quite fragile, but from experience I find I get more fish as a result. After all, even bleak become hook-shy occasionally. By using such fragile tackle I cannot knock or shake the bleak from the hook—the usual method in the Midlands. It would break if I did. But this is no disadvantage and even if I have to unhook each fish by hand I don't lose any time. The big secret of a bleak hook though is not the size but the pattern—it has to be eyed. This really is a time-saver, for the eye of the hook prevents the maggot being blown up the line and re-baiting is cut to a minimum. I reckon the angler who first discovered that was a genius.

You will have noticed by now that I always talk about the hook maggot and never mention any other bait. The reason for this is because in my experience a maggot is definitely the best bait for bleaking. Not a good soft hook maggot though, that would be wasted. It should be just the opposite. The tougher, older, and thicker-skinned it is the better, for then it will last for several fish. The bleak will continue to take even when it is just a shred of skin and I keep offering the same maggot until they refuse it. Only then do I re-bait. I remember one big match when I had some particularly tough hook maggots, about three weeks old, and I found that sometimes I was taking up to a dozen bleak without having to change the bait. I have heard of matchmen trying artificial baits in a bid to speed things up but it has never worked for me. Bleak are not that stupid. I did take a few once on a piece of wash-leather but nowhere near so many as with the genuine thing. Even when they are mad on feed and coming at every chuck (the best time for experimenting) you notice the difference immediately you try it. You find that every other cast is blank. How the bleak can tell the difference between a shred of maggot skin and a bit of wash-leather I don't know, but they can. I gave casters a try just to see what would happen and I found they were equally as good as maggots but I had to re-bait after each fish. That, of course, is fatal and cuts the number of fish per hour considerably. One of the problems that faces the 'bleaker' on the Severn is knowing when and where to go for them.

Above Stourport Bridge the bleak start to thin right out and are only found in isolated shoals from there on up to the river's source. Below the bridge, the shoals gradually start to swell until around Worcester, and down to below Tewkesbury they must be 2ft thick all across the river. The individual pitch will decide tactics on this part of the Severn, but other factors such as who is the opposition and what other species are present plus the condition of the water, will have to be considered carefully before setting up one's stall. How do you recognise a bad bleak peg? Well, bleak do not like shallow water. They like at least 2½ft to 3ft of water beneath them. A pitch too far from the main currents, such as a bay, would not hold too many either. Overhead conditions need to be right too—you need plenty of room to wield a 14ft pole, and trees are a menace. If the bank is high behind you it provides good cover but watch out for spectators. Any activity on a high bank will push the bleak too far out in midstream to catch them. The bleak will never come really close in unless there is some cover behind, such as bushes, to hide a stark outline. Once I have decided to go for bleak in a match, the first thing I do is unroll a huge sheet of polythene. I spread this out all round my pitch, right down to the water's edge, and ruffle up the edges. The idea is to trap any bleak that fall from the hook as they are swung in. The polythene covers an area of nine square yards and it works well.

I'm certain it has won me several matches through preventing dropped bleak flopping back into the water—up to 1½lb of fish at times. I always stand up when bleak fishing. Around my waist I strap a special apron with a large pocket into which I tip about three pints of maggots for a five-hour match. I feed these five or six at a time (never more otherwise the bleak will start 'boiling' on the surface and be difficult to catch) into the swim each time a bleak swings in. In other words, at the same time a bleak swings in my left arm is throwing in maggots. After a while I virtually become a 'bleak-catching machine'. To me concentration is the most important factor when bleaking. One-hundred-per-cent concentration and nothing less is vital if double figures are to be reached. Once I have started catching, I develop a rhythm and my mind is closed to everything outside my own small world. My reactions become automatic and I never miss a fish. Break that intense concentration (a spectator speaking, or a tangle) and it takes a while before I get back to the three-a-minute routine. Three a minute sounds a lot but it is easy really and sometimes I feel I could keep it up all day long. The trouble is the bleak come in bursts—the shoal is forever moving and there are many blank periods in each hour. One thing I have to watch carefully, so great is my concentration, is that I don't gradually turn towards the flow of the river. If I didn't keep checking with a marker opposite, I would finish up fishing well downstream with the bleak getting further and further away.

When I do lose the shoal, and it often happens, the first thing I do is put on a no 8 dust shot 6in from the hook and start fishing deeper. This usually finds them again but occasionally you start catching dace that have moved under the bleak and scared them off. The only other time I use any lead on my tackle is when an upstream wind holds the line and prevents the bait sinking at the correct speed. To overcome this I use micro-shot. Just one fastened a few inches from the hook will drag the maggot down at just the right speed and the bleak are no wiser. Sometimes, no matter how hard I try, I cannot contact the shoal—this happens on very sunny days and I realise they are a long way out in midstream. Only then do I use my 18ft pole. It is hard work manipulating this long pole and I have got to be really struggling before I put it together.

While Bob's general approach to bleak snatching can hardly be improved upon, several experts disagree with his method of using fine hook lengths and handling every fish. Ron Russell, who helped pioneer the Severn style, prefers to shake the bleak off the hook into the net as he reckons it saves valuable time in a match. Ron, therefore, ties slightly larger hooks to stronger line—2lb to 2½lb breaking strain—and as the bleak swings in he catches the line a foot above the fish between his index finger and his thumb, with his little finger uppermost and his palm towards the water. Then he lowers the bleak over the keep-net and gives his hand a sharp twist in an anti-clockwise direction. This swings the fish over his hand and jerks it off the hook.

So much for catching the little blighters but there are many occasions when we want to get our bait through the bleak and nearer the bottom to contact better-quality fish of other species. The answer to this is heavier terminal tackle with plenty of lead towards the hook, plus a few slices of bread or floating casters to keep the shoals right on the surface. The bread will keep the bleak occupied for long periods, and they will follow floating casters until each one has been eaten. They soon return if any loose feed is thrown in, so place all hook samples in heavy groundbait mixed and squeezed together so that it doesn't break up until it hits the bottom. But even these tactics are useless in areas where bleak are very prolific, and the only solution is to leger.

Bream

Although bream are somewhat lethargic fish, with a preference for still or sluggish water, they live quite happily in the lower reaches of the Severn. While this stretch can hardly be described as sluggish, its great depth and slower currents obviously suit the species as huge shoals haunt certain areas including the tidal waters. Bream first· begin to show in reasonable numbers downstream of Holt Fleet and gradually become more predominant as the river approaches Tewkesbury. But while small bream, or 'skimmers' as they are known, are likely to turn up anywhere between the two points, the bigger fish seem to shoal tightly in very localised spots where they remain year after year.

Most of the 'bream holes' are in the very deepest areas such as Ripple and Bushley where there is as much as 18ft of water in midstream, but there are many exceptions with no particular pattern to provide any guidelines in locating them. I suppose that, being bottom feeders, the main attraction must be a plentiful supply of natural food on the river-bed, but there is no way of finding out where these areas are.

One thing I have noticed is that bream are often found in the vicinity of bridges and surely this must be more than coincidence. On the Severn for instance, the area where the M50 bridge crosses Ripple, is a well-known bream haunt, as is that part of the river near the railway bridge at Upton. I can think of two more examples on other rivers and these are the M5 bridges across the Avon at Strensham and the Huntspill in Somerset—both these spots are noted for bream and the fish were there before the bridges were built. My own explanation for this is that as the bridges are sited on the firmest strata in the area it is highly probable that the river-bed around the bridge is hard gravel or rock which the bream must like.

Obviously, there must also be plenty of insect life such as larvae, worms, small shell creatures etc, which form the bream's natural diet. The direction of the current is important in this respect as a lot of food is washed downstream, which is perhaps why bream tend to congregate on the bends where this food is likely to settle. But, while attempting to sort out the bream holes by reading the river is difficult, the shoals often give away their position in warm weather when they roll and prime on the surface. This is always a good sign too, as rolling bream are invariably ready to begin feeding.

Another sign that bream are about, though not always easy to see on the Severn, are the bursts of small bubbles rising to the surface as they grub among the silt and mud on the river bed. Usually though, the only way to make sure of contacting a shoal is to concentrate on the well-known and proven haunts in the summer and autumn while bearing in mind that, though the shoals favour a certain area, they do move around considerably. Severn bream are mainly summer feeders and the biggest catches are taken during July, August and September.

This is not to say that they cannot be caught at other times. On the contrary, good bags are taken all through the season, even in winter if the weather is mild. Apart from the few shoals found further upstream (which I discuss elsewhere) the average Severn bream are small, scaling between 1½lb and 2½lb. Odd three- and four-pounders are hooked occasionally, but the shoal fish are usually like peas in a pod. Nevertheless, get them feeding freely and they keep coming for hours on end, as many anglers have demonstrated by netting hundredweight catches.

The summer of 1975 was a particularly good Severn bream season when 100lb hauls become almost commonplace on certain stretches. The catches came from widely separated areas such as Oak Meadows at Kempsey, Ripple, Bushley, Tewkesbury and Lower Lode on the tidal reaches. The latter venue also coughed up some huge catches in 1976 which was not a good season elsewhere. I personally witnessed one 150lb catch from upstream of the Lode Hotel. The successful baits for these mammoth bags are nearly always maggots or breadflake. Severn bream are not too fussy in this department, which is a comforting thought because if they won't accept either it is a safe bet they won't look at anything else, which can save a lot of wasted effort. Unlike other Severn species which can usually be tempted one way or another, generally bream feed or don't feed, and this applies all along the river. The pattern is quite noticeable at big matches when, if bream do not figure in the leading weights, it's a foregone conclusion that few were caught.

Because of the great depth on the lower river, plus the fact that bream like a still bait, legering is by far the best method, though the sliding float is used occasionally, mainly in the slightly shallower areas such as Severn Stoke. For legering, a 10ft rod is about the right length as this enables control over the fish and is short enough to have the tip close to hand for spotting delicate bites. Many Severn experts use a 'soft top' rod as a bite indicator, but a supple quiver tip, about 12in long, is as good as anything. Swing tips are not very satisfactory because of the strong flow.

But no matter which bite indicator is used, it is important to place the rod in two rests, facing upstream at an angle to the bank. Set this way, the angle of the line is such that the merest touches are immediately transmitted to the quiver tip or soft top. Two-and-a-half pound breaking strain reel line is quite strong enough as the chances of connecting with a big fish are remote. Also, the stronger or thicker the line the more resistance it offers to the current which means that more lead is needed to anchor the bait on the bottom.

Hook lengths can be the same strength as the reel line in coloured water, though it is often necessary to scale down to $1\frac{1}{2}$lb in clear conditions. Terminal rigs depend mainly on personal choice, though the paternoster is most widely used.

(opposite) A typical catch of bream taken from the deeper, slower moving, reaches of the river near Tewkesbury

This is normally made up with a half-ounce bomb, bullet or coffin lead, tied to a short length of nylon thicker than the reel line, which in turn is fastened to a small link swivel. The swivel is stopped by a small shot or short length of rubber tubing near the loop of the reel line and the hook length connected below it. Hook sizes depend on the bait and conditions. For maggots, in clear water, it is sometimes essential to use a size 20, though a size 16 is preferred when possible. Breadflake, of course, demands a larger hook and size 10 or 12 usually fits the bill.

When a likely pitch has been selected and the tackle set up, the first and most important step is to find the deepest area of the swim, which is where the bream are most likely to be. A favourite place is the channel washed out years ago by petrol-tankers as they plied up and down the river. This is normally, but not always, out in midstream and, though it is gradually silting up, is still quite marked along most stretches. The only way of testing the depth with leger tackle is to count as the lead sinks to the bottom—indicated by the line going slack.

Having decided on a mark, don't be in too much of a hurry to begin fishing, but first make a few trial casts to ascertain whether the river-bed is clean. The lower Severn is notorious for its snaggy bottom—sunken trees, rocks etc, litter the river-bed in places. If it is clean, the next item on the agenda is to lay a thick carpet of groundbait. Now, while cereal groundbait may have gone out of fashion along the upper reaches and the middle river, it is essential for bream and, within reason, the more you put in the better the chances of a good catch. But the operation must be carried out carefully. For instance, if the river is calm and clear, any disturbance will almost certainly scare the bream so in these circumstances it is a good policy to ladle in the groundbait all at once and then wait for the bream to come back to it.

On the other hand, if the surface is rippled (always the best conditions) groundbaiting can be carried out at intervals, but still with the accent on a large amount at the start, say at least half-a-dozen cricket-ball-sized lumps. It should be mixed really heavy too, otherwise it will float for yards before it hits the bottom. If maggot is the hook bait, plenty of squatts should be added to the groundbait as bream love these small feeders. Casters also attract them (though they are not nearly so good on the hook) and most experts include a few in the mix. Bearing in mind the strong pull of the river, the groundbait should be aimed well upstream of the mark you intend to fish. Judging the distance the groundbait will travel before it hits the bed of the river can be difficult at times, and it is something that only experience can teach. Allow at least 2yd in normal conditions, less when the river is low, and more if there is a downstream wind.

When groundbaiting has been carried out, the next problem comes in placing the hook bait on it with as tight and short a line as possible. In other words, you don't want a long bow in the line as this will weaken the bite signal. In this respect it is essential that the leger weight is heavy enough to just hold the bottom, but if in doubt it is better to fish too heavy than too light. One way of ensuring that the line is really tight at all times is to slam the bait arm on as the lead hits the water. But the drawback here is that the terminal rig falls in an arc which must be allowed for by over-casting the correct distance. The other way, and the one most favoured, is to cast just beyond the mark, leaving the bait arm open and tightening up by reeling in immediately the lead hits the bottom.

When everything has been worked out satisfactorily, bites, when they come, are usually quite positive with the quiver tip moving out an inch or so, or dropping back if the fish disturb the lead. In winter, or if the river is below par, bites are very timid and difficult to spot, and then it pays to twitch the bait slowly through the swim by winding in a turn or so at intervals. This tactic often induces a take, usually as the bait is settling. Hitting the bites at long distance in deep water calls for a long hard strike, and it also helps if the line is wound in at the same time. Smashes can be avoided by slackening the clutch of the reel beforehand.

Although legering is the most popular method for bream, they are sometimes caught on the float with a moving bait and for this style a really hefty slider, supporting at least three swan shot, is required. One old hand I know has made himself a set of huge balsas carrying as many as eight swan and he trots the middle when the wind is favourable. He catches plenty of bream, as well as chub and roach, but it is hard work. Occasionally bream can be found quite close in, especially in swims where there is 12ft or more of water. This is when the float leger comes into its own, but you need a long rod and a bulky float to hold the bait stationary. A half-inch running bullet, stopped a foot or so from the hook, is better than a string of shot and also aids casting. An excellent bait for this style is very soft breadpaste. Bream love this, but because it is easily dislodged, it can only be used for close in fishing.

Another float legering method, which once enjoyed great popularity on the lower Severn, is a style known as 'bobbing'. This gives the best of both worlds in that it is possible to leger out in midstream and yet still watch a float for bites. The float, which should be medium and very buoyant, with a small diameter ring, is simply threaded on the line and stopped from dropping on to the terminal tackle with a small dust shot. After casting, and providing pressure is kept on the line, the loose float will eventually surface in a cocked position where it can be held by manipulating the rod. The small diameter ring helps in this respect by gripping the line slightly. It also ensures that the float is not left behind on the cast to finish up at your feet. If it does lag behind as the leger weight is in flight, a few turns of lead wire wrapped round the base should do the trick. Bites with this method are signalled by a series of bobs on the float—hence the name. Although bobbing has gone out of fashion it still has its devotees, among whom well-known Birmingham angler George Taylor is outstanding. George 'bobs' to good effect both in match and pleasure fishing, but his terminal tackle these days is a swimfeeder. Although this is the first time I have mentioned this gadget for bream fishing it's not

72

because it is ineffective. Quite the contrary, in fact more and more anglers are using them.

Earlier I mentioned a 150lb catch taken from Lower Lode. Well this was made with a feeder used in conjunction with breadflake. The angler, Graham Edmunds from Coventry, simply packed the feeder with cereal groundbait and offered pieces of flake on a size 10 hook. While the lower reaches of the Severn are regarded as traditional bream waters, the species also turns up in the faster middle section much more frequently than is generally realised.

Probably because the shoals are smaller, and there is obviously less competition for food, middle Severn bream are of a much better stamp than those caught below Worcester. Whereas a four-pounder is considered a good fish for the bottom end of the river, those found upstream grow much larger. In fact, eight- and nine-pounders are not uncommon between Bewdley and Shrewsbury. To give an example, a shoal of 4lb plus bream has been resident near the wide, deep bay at the top of the Birmingham AA's Ribbesford stretch, near Bewdley, for as long as I can remember. These fish range up to 9lb and my records show that they turn up year after year, even in winter. The usual catches consist of three or four fish, but occasionally some lucky angler happens to be in the right place at the right time with the right bait (breadflake is favourite) and takes a bonanza haul—as did Archie Dalwood, secretary of the Dudley AS which leases the left bank at Bewdley. Archie contacted the shoal just below the bay one day in the summer of 1976, and landed an estimated 140lb, including an 8lb 12oz specimen, on breadflake. Archie is very familiar with this particular shoal, and he points out that he cannot remember any small bream ever being caught from this area.

The river around Bridgnorth produces many monster bream, and well-known angler, Ron Lewis, has had notable catches of fish up to 8lb. Ron, who knows this part of the Severn like the back of his hand—he has walked and swum underwater for miles to study the contours of the river-bed— maintains that there are plenty of big bream in the area but they are generally isolated in small groups in the deeper holes. Unfortunately, these marks are often full of snags and form tackle traps. So, next time you hook and lose a big fish don't be quite so certain it was a good barbel—it may well have been a double-figure bream.

Further upstream, above Atcham Bridge, near Shrewsbury, there are several known shoals, especially at Emstrey on the LMS waters, where club members think nothing of 50lb and 60lb catches. Paradise Meadows, the Severn-Trent Water Authority water, immediately above the bridge, has also yielded several eight pounders over the years. One of the biggest match catches from the Severn, consisting of bream between 3lb to 5lb and totalling 97lb, came from the top of Emstrey. The lucky captor was Lancashire angler Harry Anders, and the bait he used was breadflake. A few days later, at the same venue but well downstream, Shrewsbury match-angler 'Watty' Harris hooked what he insists was a bream in the teens of pounds. Unfortunately, the fish slipped the size 16 hook and escaped, even though Watty dived in after it. Several witnesses, including veteran Shropshire expert Ted Biddulph, confirmed the size of the fish, maintaining that it was like 'a dustbin lid'.

Although it is an accepted fact that the shoals stay in the same general area of the river year after year, locating these big bream is a chancy business. The summer is the time when they show most, without a doubt, but they frequently turn up in autumn and winter. The usual middle river bream haunts are the slow, deep waters—hardly surprising for this species—and the wide bays such as at Emstrey, Bridgnorth and Bewdley are the obvious places to try. As for bait— breadflake, as I have said, is definitely the best attractor at all times of the year, but small red worms also have their moments.

74

Chub

Chub are widely distributed along the whole river, and though the population was considerably reduced by the fish diseases of the 1960s, they are a hardy species that are returning in large numbers. The 'barbel explosion' also had a detrimental effect on the shoals in the middle reaches, forcing them from their favourite haunts. Many once-famous chub swims are sadly no more but others are becoming established, notably along the lower river. It seems that while Severn chub love fast, aerated glides and rapids they are equally at home in deep steadier water.

Gregarious creatures, chub are always together in large shoals, or small groups, and if one is hooked it is a safe bet that there are more in the vicinity. Most shoals consist of similar sized fish, probably because they stay together from the time they were spawned. Then, as the years pass, the shoal gradually thins out and the individual fish get larger, until only a few big ones remain. This theory would explain the 'like peas in a pod' type of catches that are a common occurrence at most venues. Ocasionally, however, the shoals become mixed, and when this happens the bigger chub are invariably in command at the head or lying safely at the rear.

Unlike barbel, chub like plenty of space and the shoals are often spread over large areas. It is a common sight along some of the quieter stretches in summer to see the river become black from bank to bank with basking chub. Although the shoals wander considerably, they stay more or less in the same vicinity for most of the year, even in winter, and consequently there are dozens of popular chub swims dotted along the river. In fact, almost every venue has at least one well-known hole. On the upper and middle reaches these are usually at the tail-end of fords and in the deeper pools below or in the steady shallow glides. The channels and gullies that abound in the shallower stretches also hold a large quota, particularly in the weedier areas. Those attractive swims where the main current sweeps across and down the edge of the river, such as at the top of Knowle Sands, are also favourite haunts. However, from Stourport downstream the character of the river hardly varies so the chub has little choice for its home. They are therefore not so easy to find. The most likely spots on the lower river are those where trees and bushes hang over the water's edge.

Food in the form of caterpillars, insects and various berries which drop off into the river attract the chub and so they make their home in roots and sunken branches. Chub are omnivorous and mouth anything they find in the river, consequently the list of baits that will attract them is so numerous that it would be easier to list those that don't, that is if there are any. Favourites for the Severn are: casters, maggots, breadflake and luncheon meat, but tares, wheat, hempseed, cheese and worms account for good catches on occasions. Wasp grub, when available, is another deadly chub bait and they can also be caught with artificial dry and wet flies as well as with small spinners and live baits.

Because of their catholic diet and willingness to chase any likely morsel they see, chub tend to feed at all depths in summer and winter. They often lie near the surface in warm weather waiting to chomp anything that comes floating by. At such times floating crust or bread, or indeed any bait that floats, is worth trying. In cooler weather, chub tend to keep to the bottom, especially at the beginning of a cold spell but once they have become acclimatised their need for food sets them moving again. So while a bait offered in winter on or near the river-bed is much more likely to be successful, many fish are still caught in mid-winter. Of all the species in the river, apart from grayling, chub seem to be the most adaptable to temperature changes which make them a popular quarry all year. In very cold weather they are often the only fish willing to feed, and while they don't exactly gorge themselves at such times I can recall many outings when a solitary chub has saved the day from a complete blank.

Izaak Walton described chub as the 'fearfullest of fishes' and though this is true in as much as they are easily scared by any unusual disturbance in the river or on the banks, they are not tackle-shy. In summer and autumn, when they are really greedy for food, they will accept the largest hooks and stoutest lines, but you have got to fish down the middle or even further out to catch them. This is the time when huge catches are taken. Up to 70lb in a match is not uncommon, and Wolverhampton angler Ron Baker once landed $74\frac{1}{2}$lb in three hours of a four-hour contest to set a record for the river. Pleasure hauls from well-known chub pitches often exceed this figure by a large margin and I have reported several over 100lb.

It is a different story in winter, however, and though plenty of chub are caught in the coldest months, greater care with tackle is needed and both hooks and baits need to be scaled down considerably to attract them. Probably because of their numbers Severn chub do not attain the greatest of sizes, at least not by national standards. Somewhere between 5lb to 6lb appears to be the upper limit, though one or two over 7lb have been reported over the years. The latest of these came from the Harris and Sheldon water at Arley and was landed by Birmingham angler Alan Smith. Well-known veteran George Worth brought a 7lb plus fish to the net at Newtown back in the 1950s, and in 1972 young Shrewsbury angler Derek Heathcote claimed a fish of 7lb 5oz, but this was never verified.

Although it seems unlikely that a Severn chub will ever break the record, there are plenty around the 4lb mark and fish of this size can set hearts beating faster, especially if hooked on fine tackle. Chub generally haven't a great reputation as fighters but this cannot be said about the Severn variety. They may not have the strength of barbel but they put up a dogged resistance. Hook a three-pounder in the rapids at Coalport, or well downstream of one of the fast glides below Bridgnorth, and it will be some time before it comes to the net.

The author nets a plump chub from a typical Middle Severn swim at Cressage

But beware if there are any snags around as chub are very crafty and make for the nearest patch of weed or sunken branches as soon as they feel the hook. The bigger fish rarely stray far from the shelter of such places, and if they manage to get there it's a foregone conclusion that they will escape. How they do it is a mystery, but they can transfer the hooks from their mouths or wrap the hook lengths around an obstacle in a matter of seconds. I have seen experienced anglers near to tears at one well-known snaggy chub hole at Stourport. It is called 'the sunken boat swim' for obvious reasons, and the numbers of chub that have been hooked and lost is truly amazing. The only answer to such a problem is to use really stout tackle and 'bully' the chub out without ceremony as soon as they are hooked. Unfortunately the particular shoal at Stourport are unusually shy of heavy gear, no doubt because they have been hooked and escaped so often.

One of the most deadly baits for chub is wasp grub. In

fact it is so good that most Midland associations have banned its use in matches, under the ruling that because it isn't generally available it is unfair to those competitors who cannot obtain a supply. An example of the power of 'the grub' was Ron Baker's 74½lb catch of chub made opposite the boathouse on the Quarry length at Shrewsbury. Ron had the chub (which ran to 3½lb) queuing up for the hook that day and, but for an overturned rowing boat in his swim, would surely have cracked 'the ton'. His catch, and dozens more like it, proved the end of the wasp grub in contests however, and it was banned shortly afterwards. There is nothing to prevent individual anglers trying it out though, providing they can find and dig out the necessary nests. At least five or six are required to make a session worthwhile.

One of the secrets behind the bait is the large quantity of wasp grub groundbait used to build up a shoal in a small area. It is true that odd chub can be caught with wasp grub without the use of groundbait, but to really get them going mad a large supply is necessary, and this calls for a great deal of preparation before an outing. If the groundbait is right and there are chub anywhere in the vicinity you can be sure of a fair catch. I believe, and this view is shared by many anglers, that there is some substance in wasp nests that chub just cannot resist once they get the taste. When the groundbait is introduced they seem to lose all their wariness and sometimes leap from the water to grab grubs that jerk off the hook as it hits the surface.

So how do we set about the task of obtaining and preparing the 'magic' bait? The first step is to find a sufficient number of nests, which I should add becomes easy after a little practice. Wasps are active between July and October and build their nests in all sorts of places. River banks, the edges of woods, the sides of ditches, and waste ground in suburban areas are favourite spots. The experienced 'nester' watches for homing wasps, that is those which are flying purposefully in a straight line. Any that settle or appear to be wandering aimlessly can be ignored. Anyway, follow the general direction of the wasp and eventually, if you are on the right track (bear in mind that it could be flying *from* the nest) others will be seen heading in the same direction. As you approach the nest more and more wasps will lead you to the entrance which is invariably a hole in the ground. This spot should be marked for future reference and the search continued. Often there are several nests in the same general proximity.

When it is time to remove the nests (many anglers leave them as long as possible to ensure a regular supply), the problem is how to do it without getting stung. 'Cymag', if obtainable, is by far the most efficient wasp killer but it can be dangerous, so it is better to use one of the many proprietary brands sold for the purpose. Most are in liquid form and can be applied soaked on cotton-wool, placed in the entrance last thing at night when all the wasps have returned. When you are certain that all the wasps are dead, insert a length of flexible wire as far as it will go down the entrance tunnel and dig along it until the nest is revealed. Lift it very carefully, in one piece, to avoid losing any cake or grubs. The nests consist of several layers, or 'cakes' each containing hundreds of juicy grubs or partly-formed wasps. Towards the end of the summer one cake will contain 'queen grubs' which, being much larger than average, make extra-special hook baits. The grubs for the hook are removed by gently breaking up the cakes. Two or three hundred will be required and these should be kept in dry bran.

The remainder of the cakes, nest and partly-formed wasps, should then be thoroughly scalded in a bucket. When cool the mixture is mashed and pulped until it has the consistency of porridge. This 'mess' (for the want of a better name) is the basis of the groundbait and the next step is to thicken it enough to be moulded into balls. Breadcrumbs, plus a little silver sand, is a good combination as this can be mixed like putty and is heavy enough to be thrown long distances—an important factor in most chub swims. Equipped with a bucket of groundbait and a good supply of grubs for the hook you are now ready for the fray.

Having selected a likely pitch, the next step is to introduce a few tennis-ball-sized lumps to the head of the swim, out in the middle of the river. Chub will come close in for the grubs but they can be kept interested much longer if you stay well away from the shoal—that is unless there is an exceptional depth. Normally, most chub swims on the middle reaches average between three and four feet, so it pays to fish from the middle to two-thirds across the river.

Wasp grub tackle needs to be powerful to attain these distances and a 12ft or 13ft, fairly whippy rod, capable of handling up to 40yd of line and heavy terminal tackle, is a must. Reel lines vary according to personal choice but most experts keep them as light as possible. Bewteen 2½lb to 4lb is ideal and will safely handle chub up to 5lb. Hooks need to be on the large side and there is no need to worry about scaring the chub here. A size 8 or a size 10 at the start, with a change up or down according to how the fish are feeding, is the usual practice. Floats, too, should be big and able to support as many as six swan shot. Weighty terminal tackle will aid long smooth casting (underarm is best) as any jerkiness dislodges the grubs off the hook. The shot is fastened in a bunch about 18in from the hook in accordance with conditions, and the float set so that the grubs just miss the bottom. However, chub often rise in mid-water so constant adjustment may be necessary. Three or four grubs on the hook, plus a maggot on either side to hold them in place, will ensure that at least one remains by the time the tackle has settled in the swim, but watch out for 'drop bites'. In fact, it pays to strike at any unusual float movement.

When short of hook bait try a piece of breadflake occasionally, it often attracts a better class of fish. Another good dodge is to leger a piece of 'cake' containing several grubs well down the swim. If there are any monsters about this will certainly tempt them. 'Fishing the bread', as most Severn anglers term long-trotting a substantial-sized piece of breadflake down the middle or far side of the river, is another top method for chub especially in clear water. There are many fine exponents of this style and though Fred 'The Bread' Bailey has become nationally known for his amazing catches with it, credit for first demonstrating its potential must go to Ron Lewis of Bridgnorth. Ron has used virtually no other bait than bread for many years and the knowledge he gained (and freely passed on) is now widely practised on all parts of the river. Bread fishing is a simple enough style that brings results in summer or winter, but it scores mainly when the river is low and clear.

This is how Fred Bailey describes the technique:

Basically the tackle consists of a long-shanked size 10 hook—I use an eyed pattern and I tie this direct to my 3lb reel line. I never vary the hook size, not even when the chub are mad on feed, it is always a size 10. Twelve inches from the hook I place all my shot in a bunch. Usually this is four swan shot but I do fish lighter if I come close in. Bear in mind that mostly the chub lie well out in mid-river. I set the float (always cork on quill) so that my bait just trips the bottom and I work this out by trial and error. Now for the important part—the bread. I use a piece about the size of an old penny which I pull out of the centre of a really fresh 'tin' loaf. Freshness is vital and I would never use bread over one day old. The reason for this is not the chubs' digestion but to ensure that it stays on the hook. Fresh bread stays on the hook, stale bread comes off, it's as simple as that. Anyway I pull my hook through it and squeeze it on the shank. I have had two fish on the same piece of bread many a time so I believe this to be the best way. I use a hefty overhead cast to get my bait out and my shot being all bunched together helps to prevent tangles. A big piece of bread offers a lot of resistance when casting so it is vital to use a fairly whippy rod that will stand constant punch casting. I don't hold the float in check as it travels down the swim. I prefer to let it go with the natural flow unless there is a downstream wind, then I hold back. Bites vary but, and this is essential, strike at the slightest movement of the float, don't wait for it to go under.

I strike at every unusual float movement and some of the biggest chub I have netted have come from slight lift bites. I use plenty of groundbait during a match, despite the critics who condemn its use. I believe that careful groundbaiting will keep the shoal as tight as it is possible to keep a chub shoal, but I am careful not to make too much disturbance when I am throwing it in. A golf-ball-sized piece every five or six casts seems to do the trick far better than the big cannon-balls some anglers throw in. Ordinary breadcrumb, soaked well to ensure it doesn't float, is all I use but occasionally, if I think the swim might not yield very many chub, I mix casters so that I can attract dace as well. It's a big advantage when chub fishing on the River Severn in knowing where to find them. Some parts of the river are practically devoid of chub and it's a complete waste of time fishing for them. I don't know why this is, but I know several very chubby-looking swims that never produce a fish. Often this type of pitch is found in really open water where the banks provide little cover, but it is not a hard and fast rule, for I also know tree and bush-lined lengths where the chub population is sparse. It is not always necessary to fish the middle when bread fishing, it all depends on the depth of the water. If there is 6ft close in it is possible to get them shoaled much nearer, only two or three rod lengths away, so I don't automatically fish the middle. I find my depth first and if there is sufficient water I try close in. Of course, if the water is shallow, as it often is above Stourport, you must fish the middle and sometimes well past it.

While most anglers are content to use well-soaked bread or ordinary commercial groundbait as an attractor when 'fishing the bread' Ron Lewis, doyen of the 'bread men' is much more scientific. He goes to a great deal of trouble to ensure that his groundbait is perfect for all types of swims, and it must be admitted that some of his catches appear to make the extra effort worthwhile. Ron aims for a single mixture that will not only break up at any depth he desires, but will also attract chub without overfeeding them; this is how he goes about it. Three or four stale loaves are soaked and mashed up in a bucket of water and then separated into several different bowls, each about a third full. Each bowl is then held under the full force of a cold water tap which breaks up the bread into fine particles and produces a milky residue in the water. The bowls are then left to stand until the fine particles have settled. The milky water is subsequently drained off and the process repeated. Ron's theory is that the 'milky' substance clogs up the groundbait, so for clear water he washes it all out. He is not so particular for deep strong-flowing swims however, and only washes it a couple of times.

After the washing is completed, the next step is to squeeze as much water from the bread as possible by forcing it through a fine-mesh riddle and then laying it out on newspaper overnight to dry out further. Finely-ground bread-crust is then added in the proportion of one-and-a-quarter buckets of crust to one of bread. This is mixed until the groundbait is a golden colour with a nice spongy texture. It breaks up in the river according to how hard each ball is squeezed. In shallow water a gentle squeeze is enough to hold it together sufficiently to ensure that the ball explodes near the surface, while more pressure is needed to get the ball in one piece near the bottom of fast, deep pitches.

Breadflake will also tempt chub on the surface in the summer, and Ron Russell has designed a special float for this method. It is a loaded cane and balsa pattern that holds the line above or on the surface. To make it all you need is a 4in length of $\frac{5}{8}$in diameter balsa rod, a 6in long piece of $\frac{1}{8}$in diameter cane, and a 3in round nail. The cane is inserted into the balsa, leaving 5in proud, and a small ring whipped to the tip. Push the nail into the other end of the balsa until it is flush, and you will find that it cocks the float until all the cane and $\frac{1}{2}$in of balsa protrudes above the surface. Adjustments may be made by shortening the nail or shaving the balsa. Then all that is required is a coat of paint.

The float is fastened to the line with two stop knots 3ft apart with about 5ft between the bottom knot and the hook which is tied direct. After casting, the line should be wound in until the bottom knot is forced against the float ring. This ensures that the line near the hook is above or on the surface. Now while surface fishing is possible with most ordinary floats, the advantage of Ron's model lies in the fact that chub often roll over a floating bait causing it to sink slightly before they grab it. With conventional tackle this results in false bites but Ron's float doesn't register until the chub has pulled the bait 3ft or until the top knot hits the float and tips it flat. Then is the time to strike. This method, incidentally, works with other baits besides bread and crust. Floating casters are deadly as is wasp cake.

Another method for chub (as well as barbel and other species) that brings great rewards on the shallow middle reaches is 'waggler' fishing. These floats can offer many advantages, when long-trotting shallow water with casters or maggots. For instance, because of the way they are fastened (by the bottom ring), tangling, that great bugbear of long casting, is eliminated. And with the line being partially sunk it is much easier to fish a straight line. The submerged line also cuts out surface disturbance on the strike and helps to combat a downstream wind. Furthermore, because the waggler is fished with a long tip showing (at least an inch), it is always visible even when the surface is rippled on sunny days. The style is simple enough to use but there are basic rules to follow to get the most out of it.

Firstly, the best wagglers for the Severn are plain quills with added bodies. These carry sufficient weight (up to three swan shot) and aid casting as well as striking. Secondly, the float should be locked in place on the line with two anchoring shot placed 2in apart. This gap allows the waggler to lie back on the strike, so lessening the resistance. Thirdly, a heavier line than usual, say $3\frac{1}{2}$lb instead of $2\frac{1}{2}$lb, should be used. This is to take the strain of the whipping action necessary to force the line nearest the float beneath the surface immediately after casting. It also absorbs the shock of the more direct strike which the 'peg leg' style gives. Severn wagglers are best shotted to a formula of 80 per cent of the total load each side of the float and the remainder at intervals below. A slight variation of, say 70/30, is necessary in swims over 5ft deep. An example with a float carrying $2\frac{1}{2}$ swan shot would be four AAA to lock it into place and three no 4s spread out underneath. Ideally, the method is most suitable in swims between $2\frac{1}{2}$ft to 7ft deep. In shallower water the surface is too powerful and drags the line, while in deeper swims more lead is needed nearer the hook and a conventional float fastened top and bottom would be better.

A snag with the waggler is that it cannot be held back to slow the progress of the bait, but this can be overcome to some extent by dragging the bottom providing that it is clean, or making use of an upstream wind by allowing it to bow the line. Another way is to cast downstream towards the shoal so that the bait reaches them before the float comes under the effect of the surface current. Bites with the waggler are usually positive as it doesn't take much of a pull to drag it under. Lift bites are common, especially when loose feeding, and when these become too frequent an adjustment of the shotting pattern is necessary.

Chub have a strong predatory streak which is often evidenced in summer when they gorge on small fish such as minnows and fry. When in this mood they gang up on the shoals of tiddlers, usually in the shallows, and the bow-waves they create as they attack give away their presence. At such times spinning with a small fly spoon is a deadly method, and fair catches can be taken providing there isn't too much weed about to foul up the lure. I was introduced to this method on my earliest visits to the river back in the 1950s. In those days it was common to hook trout and perch as well as chub from the fords, and my friends and I often landed good specimens of each species. There were far fewer anglers about in those days though, and we had plenty of room to work, so after hooking two or three fish we would move on in search of a big 'un. And big chub, at least for the Severn, we hooked, including plenty over 3lb.

Tackle for this method is quite simple. All that is required is a light spinning rod, a fixed spool reel loaded with 3lb or 4lb line, plus a few fly spoons, swivels and anti-kink leads. The spoon, plus swivel, can be tied direct to the reel line, or, if preferred, to a slightly weaker trace with a couple of anti-kink leads added a foot or so above. These will keep the lure down in the water and help reduce that great hazard of spinning—line twist. Small pools around the fords are the most likely places to find the chub when they are hunting fry, but a cast in the rapids often pays dividends.

The cast should be made across and downstream, the distance being determined by the nature of the surface water. If it is broken, or rippled by the wind, it is possible to approach quite near the chub. But a glassy surface calls for longer casting, unless there is a fair depth as fish can see a long way in such conditions. The spoon can be retrieved very slowly in fast currents, in fact it will spin attractively even if held stationary off the bottom. But a gentle 'sink and draw' action at varied speeds gives a more lifelike movement and is therefore even more attractive. The 'take' when it comes is quite positive and the rod tip is jerked fiercely, unless it happens to be a very small chub. Surprisingly, fish of only two or three ounces will sometimes grab the spoon.

To whet your appetitie for chub spinning, let me record the experience of Willenhall (West Midlands) angler Arthur Jones on an outing to Coalport in the summer of 1976. Arthur fancied his chances of catching a trout on a spinner from the stretch opposite the post office. But he hooked a 3lb chub first cast out, and that proved the start of a hectic three-hour session in which he landed many more similar samples. His total catch, witnessed by a local bailiff, was estimated at over 100lb.

Fly-fishing is equally productive in the summer and what is more will tempt chub in those dense, weedy, shallow runs where no other method is possible. It is not a widely practised style on the Severn, yet it is deadly in the right conditions. I witnessed a fine catch early one Sunday morning from an inches-deep swim just below Bridgnorth. The angler was Trevor Haycock, from Bilston, West Midlands, who landed well in the region of 60lb of chub, mainly around the 2lb mark, but including quite a few over 3lb. Each fish was in absolute mint condition which, considering the weedy area they came from was hardly suprising. It lies at the top of Knowle Sands in the middle of one of the most popular and hard-fished venues and it is (because of weed) a 'no go' area for the majority of anglers. Trevor, a keen fly-fisherman, however, fishes it regularly when the river is right which means low summer level, and he enjoys superb sport at daybreak and dusk.

When the level allows, he stands on the island in the middle of the river and casts almost directly upstream, not

too far, usually about 15yd, and eases his fly, a large bushy
'Palmer' pattern, over a channel among the weed fronds.
As the fly floats downstream he keeps a tight line by gently
pulling it back from the rod. A swirl near the surface as a
chub mouths the fly is the signal for an unhurried but
powerful strike. If he connects, the fish is quickly bullied to
the net before it knows what's happening. Speed is essential
in weedy water as, given half a chance, the chub will soon
escape. Trevor's powerful 9ft rod and a 3lb breaking
strain cast tied to his forward tapered line, enable him to
drag the chub downstream in double-quick time, but even
so he loses a fair number. Occasionally longer casting is
necessary and line control, to minimise drag, is then called
for.

Generally however, the delicacy of casting and line control
required when fly-fishing for trout, is wasted on chub. They
are not easily scared when they are in the shelter of weed,
and the plop of a fly landing heavily on the water soon
attracts them. Neither are they too particular about fly
patterns. Big bushy varieties such as 'Palmers', 'Zulus' and
'The Coachman' seem to be the most popular at Bridgnorth,
but there is plenty of scope for experiment in this field.
Trevor always uses a dry fly, but again it is not essential to
keep it floating. The day I watched him, the fly frequently
sank out of sight but it didn't deter the chub. If a boat is
available, fly-fishing can also be rewarding on the steadier,
deeper stretches where the chub lie beneath overhanging
trees. There are dozens of such places along the Severn,
many of them inaccessible from the bank but where a
stealthy approach with a fly from a boat would obviously
bring rewards in the shape of big, fat, lusty chub.

An excellent, though rarely used, summer method for
catching solitary big chub, which I have used successfully
along the upper reaches, is the float-fished minnow. I don't
know whether it is generally known but in the rocky boulder-
strewn stretches of the river where natural food is not so
plentiful, minnows form a large part of the chub's diet.
Therefore they make a first-class bait. Offering them singly

or in pairs, I have tempted dozens of 3lb chub and many over 4lb. In fact, it is such a good method that it has never ceased to surprise me that more anglers don't use it. It works best on the small pools and holes at the end of fast runs and stickles, spots which invariably hold one or two sizeable chub. But it is a 'roving' style and to cover all the likely chub haunts along a lengthy stretch calls for a great deal of walking and wading, so tackle must be as as light and as simple as possible. A 12ft fairly powerful rod with 3lb breaking strain reel line, and a short buoyant float capable of supporting a couple of swan shot as well as one or two minnows, is ideal for most swims.

Catching enough minnows for a day's sport is child's play and these can be carried in a plastic bucket or a large bottle. The chub are never fussy whether they are alive or dead providing they are reasonably fresh. Hook them through the upper lip on a size 8 or 10 which can be tied direct to the reel line, and set the float so that they just trip bottom. Shot is required to hold the minnows down and should be placed between 6in to 12in above the hook, depending on each particular swim. The buoyant float will drag the minnows down through the shallows and into the pools, but sometimes because of snags it is necessary to cast well downstream directly over the target. Two or three runs through each pool or hole, working the minnows as slowly as possible, is generally sufficient to attract any chub that may be lurking there as, if they are in the mood, they grab the minnow as soon as they spot it. Then, because of the disturbance, is the time to move on elsewhere.

While float and swimfeeder tactics account for most Severn chub in good condition, the leger often comes into its own when the river is below par. A rise in level due to rain, an influx of dam water, a change in air temperature—especially that of a cold spell, strong east winds, all upset the river's fish population but none more so than the chub. Sensitive creatures, any sudden change is likely to upset them. When this happens they become reluctant to move off the river-bed and lose their zest for hunting food. Fortunately,

Fig 8 Legering for chub – four rigs: **A** is normal swan shot leger; **B** is the Arlesey bomb fished on paternoster links

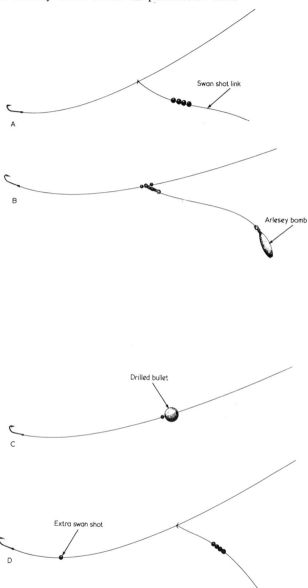

Fig. 9 **C** is drilled bullet rig and stop shot; **D** is swan shot link with extra swan shot in hook length to keep bait firmly anchored

the chub's appetite is never entirely subdued and they can be tempted with small baits well anchored on bottom in the poorest conditions. Legered luncheon meat certainly attracts chub at such times. So much so that many anglers now specialise with it throughout the winter. Some have made a name for themselves in match circles with several big wins and placings, men like Les Crook, Bert Andrews, Arthur Searle, and Ron Lees. The techniques they have developed have almost revolutionised winter chub fishing, and they also work in summer.

Let us have a look at the style used by Ron Lees. Ron is adamant that there is nothing hit-or-miss about his methods, no matter how poor the river. This is what he says:

The reverse is true as I always aim to shoal the fish, not easy when the Severn is up and coloured. Yet it is possible to get the fish together even when the river is in full spate. First you must ignore the old theory that fish move under the banks to find shelter when the river rises—it's not true.

Neither is it true that the sediment in the coloured river puts them off feed. I catch plenty of chub when the river is like cocoa. Bearing this in mind, I begin operations in a line directly in front of me and fairly close to the far bank. As soon as my leger hits the water, I slam the reel handle to tighten up and then allow the lead to drag a little until it eventually holds bottom. It is usually held up by some small object such as a pebble, a clump of weed or a twig—it doesn't take much to stop my specially designed leads from rolling. Let me explain that these legers are an oval dome-shape, but pointed at each end, with a flat bottom and sharp, flat sides. I attach them to my paternoster link by a loop of wire inserted into the lead as I make them. Of course, if the lead gets stuck in a really bad snag this spot must be avoided by a shorter cast. It would be asking for trouble to cast beyond it. Assuming the lead has found its resting place, the next step is a quick strike to shake the meat off the hook—the start of my ground-baiting programme. To speed this up I sometimes thread several small cubes of meat on the line above the hook and strike the lot off at once. Accurate casting is necessary to concentrate the meat offerings in as small an area as possible. I never throw in any loose pieces, all my feeding is done with the terminal tackle and I am very careful not to overdo it as I suspect that meat is a very filling bait. Eventually, if I am lucky, the chub will move in.

But it's difficult to hold them in the baited area for any length of time as, no matter how accurate the groundbaiting, the shoal invariably drops down the swim. I reckon there are two reasons for this. The first is due to missed bites which leave the bait in the fish's mouth to be immediately disgorged in fright or shock. Because the meat is in the fish's mouth for some time before the bite registers, it comes out in particle-form and the shoal follow this 'cloud' downstream. The other reason is the shoal's natural caution at seeing their mates disappearing or being whisked away. When the shoal first move in on the meat, sport is usually hectic with bites coming at the rate of one every two minutes. But this mad period rarely lasts longer than an hour-and-a-half and often it's much less. One disadvantage of luncheon meat is the number of bites I miss on certain occasions. It's a problem I have yet to solve but I reckon it's due to the fact that on some days the chub take the bait in a different manner—but why? Is it because something is wrong with the presentation, or are the chub not really hungry and only pecking at the bait? I don't think any of these reasons is the answer, because, for one thing chub are nearly always hungry, and as for presentation—there can't be much wrong with it as it works well enough on most occasions. All forms of legering need concentration but a little extra effort is necessary when luncheon meat fishing in poor conditions. This is because the bites are sometimes difficult to hit and usually only come at long intervals.

This is why I always stand up to leger, holding my rod at the ready. I know it can be hard work over long periods but it gives me a better chance of hooking fish than when using a rest. Although I keep an eye on my small quiver tip for bites, I also feel for them by holding the line. The reason for this is that they are sometimes transmitted up the line without the tip moving. These 'buzz' bites, as I call them, are a sort of trembling sensation which give the first indication that a fish has picked up the bait. Actually I think they are caused by the fish sucking the bait, and it's surprising how many are hooked if the strike is made at this time, or better still when the buzzing stops. Wait for this moment and you increase your chances of connecting. Another early bite indication is when the tip straightens and the fish moves the lead. But for heaven's sake don't wait for a hard pull on the rod tip. You can hook fish when this happens, but I've come to the conclusion that this pull is not a bite—it's the result of fish taking fright. Look at it this way. To move the rod tip 6in, while taking into account the bow in the line, the fish must move the bait at least 18in and I don't think for a minute that it does that just to swallow a bit of meat. More likely it picks up the meat, feels the hook or the lead, flicks its tail and is away with the bait still in its mouth when the rod is jerked. These are those 'unmissable' bites which cause a lot of head-scratching among meat anglers.

But feel the bite before the pull and you will greatly increase your chances of making contact on the strike. A tip worth mentioning at this stage, is to point the rod at the lead once it has settled and strike straight up in a vertical position. I prefer a closed-face reel and I leave this in the free-running position, holding the line in the crook of my finger. This way bites can be sensed quite easily and the finger acts as a cushion on the strike. If the reel is left in the lock position, the pick-up button becomes a potential line smasher. This has happened to me a couple of times when I have put the rod down for some reason and had a bite. When it comes to hook sizes for meat fishing, I reckon it's best to try and keep a balance with the size of the fish likely to be encountered. In this respect, I think it unnecessary to go below a size 8 for fish over 2lb. On the other hand, when the small fish are around it is sometimes advantageous to scale down to a size 12.

It is difficult to fault Ron Lees' method, but many other top anglers have very different ideas on the leger rig. Former Severn champion Les Crook is a leger specialist, whose consistency is a byword in match circles. One of his favourite terminal tackles is a sliding swan shot link together with an extra swan shot on the main line a few inches from the hook. He adjusts the rig until the shot near the hook just holds the tackle in place. Then, when a fish picks up the bait this anchor shot is disturbed which allows the leger rig to swing round in the current, which in turn releases the tension on the line, so giving a 'drop back' bite. There is no mistaking this signal and Les is usually well into the strike before the rod tip has stopped moving. He likes a good-sized hook such as a 4 or 6 tied to 4lb line, and usually searches the whole of the river in front of him with luncheon meat, meat paste, or sometimes bread—as when he won the Severn Championship.

93

Dace

How fashions change in angling. I can remember the time when dace were a popular quarry all along the middle and upper reaches of the river. They turned up in practically every swim—shallow, deep, fast and slow—and most anglers were happy to pit their wits against their wily ways and lightning bites. But new methods and techniques have changed all that. Bigger fish of other species are now being sought, and the darting dace is virtually ignored except by match-anglers at certain venues. The fish disease of the 1960s, which greatly reduced the dace population also played a part in the demise of dace fishing. Indeed, the species disappeared completely along miles of river.

Now that they are gradually returning, a new generation of anglers dismiss them in favour of barbel, chub and roach. This is a pity as dace fishing calls for considerable skill, at least to bag a large quantity. Severn dace are generally on the small side, averaging five or six to the pound. Cock fish, around the $\frac{1}{2}$lb mark, are caught now and again all along the river but you must go upstream to the higher reaches to find the bigger samples. Above Newtown, where perhaps there is less competition for food, dace from between 12oz to 14oz are not uncommon. Many in excess of this weight are reported from time to time, but it is my belief that these specimens are probably small chub. Inexperienced anglers are often confused by large dace and small chub, but there is an acid test and that is the shape of the anal fin. That on a dace is concave while the chub's is convex. Remember the phrase 'dented dace' and you can't go wrong.

Dace swim in shoals and there are often scores of these self-contained groups along certain stretches. They rarely intermingle or join forces except when attracted to the source of food trickling into the river in large quantities, for example when an angler is feeding a swim. When this happens several shoals may be attracted to the same spot. Dace love swift-running water in the summer which is why they are invariably found in and around fords. This does not necessarily mean that they are averse to the more gentle and deeper currents. There is a large head at Stourport, for instance, and although nowhere near as numerous, from here on downstream dace appear regularly in odd swims as far as the tidal reaches.

Sporting fish, they fight well on light tackle and their shy, quick bites that come only when the bait is presented properly, are often hard to hit. I can recall many frustrating hours when the maggot has come back chewed or the caster sucked dry time after time, without the slighest indication on the float. And it has made little difference no matter how I adjusted the tackle or changed methods. Eventually I learned the secret of placing a shot very near the hook, which made bites more positive and improved my catches enormously. But even this ploy isn't always successful. Dace, when in shy or slightly reluctant mood, can be very testing and can bring the temper of the most placid angler to the boil.

But attempting to find the answer to these problems is surely one of the joys of angling. Certainly, there is a great deal of satisfaction to be gained from finding a way to outwit dace. What makes dace fishing so difficult at times is that in clear, steady water they seem to be able to spot the smallest hook and finest line. They sometimes grab every offering you throw at them except the one on the hook. But if they take that they mouth and eject it so quickly that the bite never registers. Dace also have a habit of swimming downstream with the bait in their mouths at the same speed as the current. While doing this they can suck a maggot dry without so much as moving the hook length, let alone the float.

But in swift currents, or coloured steady water, it's quite a different story. When they are feeding in earnest in really brisk-paced swims, they haven't time to inspect the bait so that they suck in everything that looks like whatever they happen to be feeding on and eject anything they don't like. When the water is coloured they cannot see the tackle so easily and again they tend to take the bait without hesitation, even in slack pitches. Of course, if the colour is too thick they cannot see the bait either, so the ideal is just enough tinge in the river to camouflage the line. Sport can be fast and furious for hours on end at such times. Catch the river with 'a drop on' and slightly coloured, and dace become fairly easy to hook. On such days, in fast water, maggot is often the best bait as several fish can be taken on the same one. Building up a shoal of dace to the extent where you can almost get them feeding from your hand is possible with regular offerings of hook bait samples. They are not shy of moving very close in and will come to casters or maggots like chickens to the corn tin.

But manipulating the shoals is an art that only comes with experience. One of the best Severn dace anglers of all time, the late Alf Massey, was a master at extracting the maximum quantity of fish with a minimum of bait. In his heyday, he once caught 30lb of dace in a four-hour contest at Cressage with just one pint of maggots. The secret behind this sort of catch lies in attracting and holding the shoal beneath the rod tip. This can be done in water only 2ft deep providing there is some colour in the water or a ripple on the surface to give cover.

But even in the best dace swims on the river you must be able to judge the speed of the current sufficiently to know when and where to throw in just the right amount of feed at the correct intervals. Throw in too much too soon and the dace move downstream with the bait or become overfed. Chuck in too little at too long intervals and you may lose them completely. But get everything just right and the shoal, or shoals, will come up and stay where you can hook them at every cast—just beyond the rod end. Occasionally in the summer, when they get really hungry, dace come right on the surface to meet the loose offerings. Then the water 'boils' as they swirl among the bait. When this happens the only solution is to stop loose feeding immediately and place the casters or maggots in heavy groundbait that doesn't break up until it hits bottom. The groundbait will reduce the number of fish you catch, but there is no other way unless you are prepared to fish the surface. 'Boiling' dace are extremely difficulty to hook and the only successful method is with bleak tackle and techniques.

Generally, tackle for dace should always be as fine as possible even when the river is coloured. Float tactics are best for big bags, and the rod should be light and long enough to enable perfect float control. A 12ft or 13ft hollow glass or carbon-fibre match rod with a fast-striking tip is ideal. Reels are a matter of personal choice as there is no need for long casting—the main essential being that the line should run off very smoothly. Many anglers prefer a centre pin for close-in fishing and there's no doubt that this type has its advantages for really tight line control. Reel lines of $1\frac{1}{2}$lb to 2lb breaking strain are quite strong enough, while hook lengths should vary according to how the dace are taking. In steady, clear water 1lb bottoms may be called for, but if you can get away with something stronger so much the better. Hooks should be on the small side as dace can be infinitely hook-shy on occasions, so a size 18 or a size 20 are often necessary. But in fast, or coloured water they will sometimes accept size 14s quite readily.

Floats need to be sensitive and trimmed down in the water until only the merest 'pimple' protrudes. Even then some bites will go undetected. Stick floats are excellent on smooth-flowing steady swims, but for the swifter runs something more buoyant is required. In this respect it is again a matter of personal choice as there are dozens of different types on the market. Slim balsa-bodied models are popular, but what-ever you use, always ensure that the tip is painted in two different colours to aid the detection of a 'drop' or 'lift' bite. A white ring painted a quarter-of-an-inch below a red or black tip takes some beating.

In good conditions the float is best fastened top and

bottom, but if there is a strong downstream or cross wind the line will have to be sunk by fastening it to the bottom ring only. The latter method is less effective and many bites will be missed, but this is unavoidable. The float should always follow the feed down the swim and be kept in check or held back slightly to give an instant signal. The best way is to slow the bait down to about half the speed of the river, but remember that when the float is held back the hook rises off the bottom. Increasing the distance between the float and the bait compensates for this, but it should be done a few inches at a time until the bites are coming regularly. Bites are more positive when the bait is just off bottom but dace are always on the move so experiment at all depths.

In weedy water, a long tail between the hook and the first shot, with the float held well back, will help stop snagging. It also helps if the hook is buried deep in the caster—obviously the best bait in such swims. Bites are indicated in various ways so watch out for any unusual movement of the float and strike immediately. Often the tip merely trembles, sometime it slows down or stops moving for an instant. Then again it may inch gently sideways, lift slightly, or run downstream. In fast water it pays to keep striking all down the swim whether a bite is indicated or not. Of course, this is only possible when maggot is the bait as anything else will fly off the hook. Occasionally bites won't come no matter how hard you try. This is the time to pull the float up well over-depth to let the bait drag on bottom. This will often do the trick, especially in fast water, no doubt because the fish want the bait slowed down, or they can feel the resistance of the tackle.

Shotting—the amount and the pattern, varies according to the character of the swim—but the basic rule for dace is to keep it light and simple. In steady water dust shot may be required to help offer a slow-falling bait, while for the powerful faster currents BB shot are necessary. Generally speaking, the fewer the shot the better, and the ideal would be just one, placed, say 9in or 12in from the hook. Unfortunately, conditions on the Severn rarely allow us this luxury.

Favourite baits for Severn dace are casters and maggots, but hempseed, stewed wheat, tares, punched bread and small red worms are worth trying. Whatever is used, a good supply of loose offerings is a must in the summer. Little and often is the drill so that there is a constant trickle running down the swim. At least half-a-dozen maggots or casters at every cast are necessary to hold the shoal; and when they are coming fast the rate should be speeded up even more. Casters are tops in steady water, and used in conjunction with hempseed feed, account for many huge catches. But when throwing in hempseed beware of 'shot' bites caused by the dace grabbing the split shot in mistake for the seeds. This can be very frustrating at times and the only solution is to keep shotting to an absolute minimum or to use a strand of lead wire twisted around the line. An advantage of casters over maggots is that larger hooks can be completely buried in the husk thus increasing the chances of connecting on the strike. On the other hand, get the dace going well on maggots and, as I said earlier, you can often tempt several fish without changing the bait.

Stewed wheat is not widely used on the Severn but I have caught plenty of dace with it during the summer. And what is more, they were good fish. Its only disadvantage is that it tends to fill them up too quickly and this is difficult to avoid as you have to throw plenty in to get them feeding in the first place. Unlike chub, dace don't like cold water and as winter approaches they become less inclined to move around. Although never straying far from their usual summer haunts they tend to lie in the deeper holes or among the weed-beds of the more placid swims. They do feed in winter but in a half-hearted manner, so patience is required to get them interested. Loosefeed should be kept to as little as possible and small hooks are imperative. Float techniques work in deep water, but if the bait cannot be slowed right down, a light leger or swimfeeder rig is more successful.

Eels and Elvers

Despite the Severn's large annual migration of elvers, the adult eel population has declined in recent years. This is evidenced by the diminishing catches of the professional eel-trappers along the lower reaches and the uncertain sport experienced by individual anglers. Not that there are many eel enthusiasts among the Severn's large army of regular visitors. Most anglers, in fact, despise eels as bait-stealing, tackle-tangling, slimy pests. Those hooked accidentally are stamped unmercifully into the ground or have their heads chopped off in order to retrieve swallowed hooks. Yet while small eels, or 'bootlaces' as they are known, can be a terrible nuisance when bream fishing, big ones offer a challenge second to none when hooked on reasonably light tackle.

Unfortunately, the better-quality eels normally feed in darkness which rules out much of the river as most associations and clubs forbid night fishing. Where it is allowed, there is nothing better than a freshly killed bleak or stone loach to tempt them. I learned this from a veteran Shropshire angler at Ironbridge. I met him early one summer morning when I arrived at daybreak to bag one of the best chub and roach swims in the area. But, to my dismay, I found it already occupied by the old man. Disappointed and frustrated beyond words after travelling 30 miles specifically to fish this particular pitch I grunted. 'Doing any good?'

'Aye, I've had a few,' he replied, 'but I'm packing up now.' My disappointment turned to elation at these words and I suddenly felt quite chatty and benevolent.

'Take your time, I'm in no hurry,' I lied as I was itching to start.

'No, they've gone off now and it's time I was off too,' he said. And with that he lifted up a rod that looked like a whittled-down broom handle, wound in his line (as thick as sugar string) and stood up to dismantle the crude tackle. When I saw a small dead fish on the end of his line the penny dropped and I realised he had been eeling: 'Any big 'uns?' I asked.

'One or two,' he replied as he opened his old army haversack to reveal a mass of wriggling black eels. There must have been at least a dozen and all were at least 2lb, with a couple around the 3lb mark. Fascinated, I then learned they had all fallen for dead bleak and stone loach. The man explained how he found the loach under stones on the ford further upstream, a spot he found that also produced its quota of eels. I was surprised to learn this as, until then, I had always believed that eels preferred deep water. But, according to the old fellow, eels often move into the shallows on summer nights and fords are good places to catch them. I cannot say that I have taken advantage of his advice as my eeling expeditions are few and far between, but he obviously knew his eels so I have no qualms about passing on the information.

Pin-pointing the more usual eel venues along the river is tricky as they are likely to turn up just about anywhere, except in the very fast runs. Certainly there are few favoured spots on the lower reaches and tidal waters, but on the middle and upper river the deeper, steady lengths and holes offer first-rate chances. Here I should add that although eels feed mainly at night, quite a few are landed in the daytime from these stretches by anglers legering for chub and barbel. Salmon fishermen legering lobworms in the pools below fast runs and weirs also hook enough to suggest that these are also obvious eel haunts. Indeed, the weir pools of Tewkesbury, Diglis and Shrewsbury have yielded some of the biggest eels ever landed from the river, and I have no doubt that if night fishing were allowed they would produce many more.

Because of the eel's great strength and fondness for snaggy bottoms tackle must, of course, be strong and line of at least 5lb to 7lb is necessary to haul them out quickly. Although the species are not tackle-shy, they have very small mouths

101

so the bait and hook should be kept to a reasonable size. It should also be presented as still as possible, so leger tackle is called for. A 2in or 3in bleak, or a couple of lobworms, is large enough to discourage 'bootlaces' yet small enough to be picked up easily by better-class fish. The bait can be offered on a single size 6 or size 8, or on a treble hook tied direct to the reel line (or, if preferred, a wire trace). While worms can be impaled any-old-how, a dead fish is best offered by threading the line through it and out from the mouth before tying on the hook which, incidentally, should be inserted through the top or bottom lip.

While eels are not put off by thick line, they will soon drop a bait if they feel any resistance, so particular attention must be paid to the leger rig. The lead should be as light as possible and stopped well away from the bait. When deadbaiting you can ensure that the fish stays on the bottom by puncturing the swim bladder. Bites are usually indicated by a series of 'plucks' and then a long pull as the eel swims away with the bait.

Elvers

A fascinating feature of the Severn is the annual elver migration when billions and billions of baby eels make their way up the river. The tiny transparent creatures which have travelled thousands of miles from the Sargasso Sea, enter the river in late March and, for a few weeks, form a broad black ribbon several miles long as they battle against the currents. The column is broken up by the first weir at Tewkesbury, but below it they are caught by the thousand in peculiarly-shaped nets designed hundreds of years ago. 'Elvering' is a traditional craft but whereas our forefathers caught them for the pot, the present-day harvest usually finds its way to an elver collecting station near Gloucester from where they are exported all over the world.

The elvers only swim upstream on certain days and nights when conditions suit them. If there is fresh water in the river, or if the tide isn't right, they rest on the bottom. The art of 'elvering' is judging just when they will start to swim and where they are likely to be at a given time. Armed with this knowledge, the experts go into action and sometimes take hundredweights at a time in a good season. The Haw Bridge area, near Gloucester, is very popular, and sometimes during the run I have seen the river bank as busy there at 2 a.m. on a cold March morning as on the opening day of a new season. The catchers, many of whom are keen coarse anglers, use a large fine-gauze net, shaped like an elongated scoop, which they hold in the river against the current while the elvers swim into it. Gloucester anglers call a netful of elvers a 'shut', and another quaint name 'vump' is used to describe the foam created by the baby eels as they wriggle in a solid mass.

Apart from being a great table delicacy, elvers are also an excellent bait for many species of fish. Chub are particularly fond of them and huge bags are taken below Tewkesbury early in the season. Hooked either singly or in pairs, in the head or tail, they wriggle most attractively to tempt good-sized fish. Float or leger tactics are suitable. A late run of the little wrigglers in 1975 happened to coincide with the early weeks of the new coarse season, and many anglers made the most of the opportunity to bag catches in excess of 100lb.

In recent years, the elver run has declined somewhat which has led the Severn-Trent Water Authority to consider introducing some kind of restrictions on netting them. A close season, limiting the number of days when netting can be carried out, is on the cards. At present, anyone can go to the river and help themselves to as many as they can carry away, which may explain why the adult eel population in the Severn catchment area is not what it used to be. Eels are not greatly loved, except by a few specialists, nevertheless the decline of any species is cause for concern. Eels are scavengers and as such play an important part in the ecology of the river by helping to keep the bottom clean.

Grayling

Severn anglers are fortunate in that the higher reaches of the river support a fair head of grayling. This comparatively rare-for-the-Midlands fish thrives in the fast-flowing sparkling waters above Welshpool, and a few turn up at odd spots as far downstream as Berwick, near Shrewsbury. A beautiful fish, the grayling is related to the salmon and trout family as signified by its adipose fin. But because it spawns in the spring it is regarded as a coarse fish. Grayling, in fact, are treated as vermin on many trout fisheries, notably in the South. But why, defeats me as, besides being a very sporting fighter, they are handsome and very good to eat. Certainly they are not unwelcome in the Severn as there is a proposed new bylaw that forbids keeping grayling in keep-nets in order to help preserve them.

Probably because of their Ice Age ancestry, grayling are undaunted by the coldest weather and will feed freely in really icy water which makes them an attractive proposition in winter. I have had many good catches on bitterly cold days when the edges of the river were ice-fringed and rod rings constantly frozen. It may be my imagination, but I reckon that the colder it is the better a hooked grayling fights. And how they struggle, with an unmistakable series of sharp backward tugs on the line as they are being wound in. They make this unique movement with the aid of their huge dorsal fin, using it like a sail or rudder in the current.

In the net, a grayling is a handsome sight with its silvery ridged flanks flecked with greeny-gold and purple tints, and topped by that magnificent dorsal fin. This beautiful colouring, plus their fresh faint smell of cucumber, makes them an attractive quarry. The idea that anyone could regard such fish as vermin seems incredible.

My first contact with the species was on the river below Llanidloes on what is now Warrington AA water. There, in a boulder-strewn pool just below the railway bridge, I hooked a half-pounder on my first visit to the area. It, and several others, made a welcome change from chub and dace and I have been a grayling fan ever since. They are not difficult to catch on the whole, though obviously, like other species, they have their off-days when nothing seems to tempt them.

The big snag in grayling fishing on the upper Severn is finding them, as they tend to shoal tightly in small areas, especially in the winter. Also, the shoals keep on the move so that you can never rely on finding them in the same swim two weeks running. I recall one particular day when, after netting a double-figure haul from that railway-bridge pool at Llanidloes, I couldn't wait to go there again the following Sunday. But, though conditions were exactly the same and I used the same tackle and baits, all I caught were dace. In fact I don't think I hooked any more grayling from that swim for many weeks afterwards.

The best way to locate shoals in winter is to roam along the river exploring the fast runs, deep pools and smooth glides with a good supply of maggots or casters and light float tackle. Maggot is a favourite winter grayling bait and a constant trickle through the swim will be sure to attract any that are in the vicinity. In summer the job is made much easier as grayling feed a great deal on flies and other surface insects, so it is not unusual to see a dozen or more dimples on the surface at the same time as grayling rise to a hatch.

For bait, fishing double or single maggots on a size 16 hook supported by a slim balsa or stick float and set so that the bait bumps along the bottom, is a deadly method in smooth-flowing swims. A sprinkling of maggots or casters at frequent intervals will keep a shoal interested long enough to build up a respectable bag. For broken, shallow water (often preferred by the grayling) a short, stubby balsa float will allow better control and, important, be easier to see. 'Billy Lane' Trent trotting floats are ideal for this type of swim. Forget those bulbous traditional grayling floats sold in the shops as they are too bulky and what is more create a lot of surface disturbance on the retrieve. Not that grayling are likely to be scared by any splashing of the tackle. In fact, they are not particularly tackle-shy in fast water. In this respect it is possible to get away with quite strong hook lengths, though I always reckon 1½lb breaking strain is quite stout enough and doesn't have an adverse effect on the behaviour of the bait as does thicker nylon.

The same can be said for hook sizes. Grayling will accept quite large hooks when feeding freely, but a smaller hook will always bring more bites. As the average Severn grayling range around the 12oz mark, a size 16 is quite big enough; however if there are any bigger fish about, a size 14 hook would obviously be better. One of the best Severn grayling I have heard of for many years, a fish just under 2lb, was taken on a size 18 hook with a single caster from near Newtown in 1976. On the days when the grayling are not very active, laying-on tactics (the same as for roach) are the drill. With the float pulled up well over-depth and one or two extra shot on the hook length, the bait can be worked down the slower water on the edges of fast, deep runs, or in the pools below. Although this is a waiting game, it often produces a fish or two when any amount of trotting has failed.

Many good grayling haunts on the upper river are impossible to float-fish because of turbulence, obstructions, or very shallow water. But don't ignore them, try a light leger. Grayling can be caught with this method and I have even known them grab a lump of legered breakflake intended for chub. They give a good thump on the rod tip when they pick up the bait which makes bite spotting fairly easy. The leger link need not be heavy. A sliding link with two or three swan shot lightly pinched on, will hold bottom in most swims at short distances. This rig is also advantageous in as much as if it gets snagged among the rocks or boulders, a sharp pull frees the line from the lead shot which can then be replaced.

Small red worms make a good leger bait but maggots and casters are equally successful. Dry fly-fishing is good fun in summer and autumn as grayling are free risers, though they sometimes miss the fly in their haste to grab it. When this happens don't be afraid to try again and again until they take it as, unlike trout, they will keep rising to a particular pattern even if it is nothing like the flies they happen to be feeding on. 'Red Tags' are very popular on the Severn but grayling have been known to take all sorts of trout patterns. Wet fly is also effective, especially in winter on a nice bright day when the river is clear. 'Red Tags' again, or a 'Peter Ross' fished across and downstream in the pools below fast runs, or down the margins of quieter swims, often attract better-quality fish.

Pike

The pike potential of the Severn is virtually untapped as only a few specialist anglers hunt them. Yet the river holds a good head along most of its length, far more I am sure than is realised. The numbers that are hooked and lost by match-anglers is a pointer to the river's pike population, and most salmon anglers can tell a tale or two about the many times they have had their hopes raised only to find a pike on the end of their spinners. Looking through my records for details of Severn pike, I am amazed that so few are reported. It seems that Midland anglers regard them as a nuisance rather than a worthwhile quarry. 'I was doing great until a ruddy great pike moved into my swim, it even grabbed my keep-net,' is a common story heard on the river bank. I have experienced this several times myself, so now I always carry a few snap tackles in my basket in readiness for a bit of extra sport.

Mind you, pike can be landed on ordinary fine tackle, given a modicum of luck. I remember one occasion (while dace fishing the upper river at Llanidloes) when I spotted a large pike lying a yard from the bank in the shallow water in front of me. Out of curiosity I decided to drop my next fish in front of its nose, just to see what would happen. As I was using a size 18 hook tied to 1½lb line, I never thought that I might land it. Anyway, I hung a small dace right in front of the pike which it grabbed immediately. 'This should be interesting', I thought, as I slackened my clutch and slowly tightened up. I could still see the pike with the dace in its mouth, but as soon as it felt the slight pressure it moved in a leisurely way out into midstream. I let it go and then began to wind in as gently as possible. Much to my surprise the pike came too, until it saw me, then it shot off again. After this had happened several times, the pike got fed up with the game and ejected the dace like a shot from a gun, right at my feet. 'That's the end of that,' I thought, but to my amazement my line was still firmly attached and so the leisurely battle continued. One single shake of its head and the pike could have been free, but eventually I dragged it over my net and quickly heaved it on to the river bank where it pulled my spring-balance to 14lb.

Obviously, I was very lucky as Severn pike are not normally quite so docile. In fact, they usually fight like demons and I have been smashed many times when dace or roach fishing. I reckon these two species are their favourite dish, though they also like chub and small bream. On the upper reaches they are not averse to a grayling. Barbel they don't like, at least I have never heard of one being taken. And, significantly I think, the pike population seems to have diminished along the popular barbel stretches. Take Knowle Sands, below Bridgnorth, as an example. Before the barbel explosion this area was a well known pike haunt that regularly produced fish up to 20lb. But not any more, at least I haven't heard of any good catches for close on seven or eight years.

Finding pike in the Severn is not too difficult, providing there is plenty of room for roaming around. You have to search out their lairs, usually in the deeper water, while at the same time bearing in mind that they may not be in a feeding mood. Venues where there is a good head of fry are obviously the best areas, and there are plenty of such places along the river. Some of the best pike holes are around the mouths of tributaries, brooks and small streams, especially where a bay or backswim has been scoured out by the currents. Pike seem particularly fond of these areas, and one of the best bags I have ever witnessed came from the mouth of the Worfe above Bridgnorth. That day two Wolverhampton anglers (using roach live baits) landed seven fish between 10lb and 20lb and lost several more. The big bay at Tern mouth at Atcham frequently reveals big pike—a twenty-nine-pounder was landed a few seasons ago. Another noted spot is the bay above the Cound Lodge Hotel at Cressage. The river at Montford Bridge, above Shrewsbury, has always been famous, for its pike range up to 20lb, and I could name countless other venues that regularly yield a few monsters.

In general, pike are likely to turn up anywhere where there are roach or dace. The upper river is good pike country but the lower reaches also have their moments. Severn Stoke, Upton and Bushley, are good, as is Lower Lode on the tidal length. The weir pool at Tewkesbury is a real 'hot spot' where scores of fish up to 20lb are taken. Comparatively speaking, the majority of Severn pike that are caught are small, but there are some real monsters in the river. I have already mentioned the twenty-nine-pounder landed at Atcham, while the best on record was a thirty-four-pounder taken in the summer of 1976 from Bevere, above Worcester.

Most of these big pike fall for live-bait which is, by and large, the most productive method especially when searching strange water. Remembering that pike like to lie in quiet backwaters or lay-bys on the edge of the main current when not actually attacking the shoals, the best way to find them is to trot a live or dead bait slowly downstream about a foot off bottom, letting it swing in towards the bank at various points. Pike bungs are not much use for this style of fishing, a tapered balsa capable of supporting a reasonable-sized fish (4oz as a good average) plus a few swan shot or barrel leads to hold the bait down, is much better. Fitted with two rings, with one near the top, these floats can be used for all depths with the aid of a nylon stop knot. The bait behaves more naturally if it is suspended by a single or treble hook through the top lip but, if big pike are expected, a treble inserted in front of the dorsal or pelvic fin can also be added. Mounted this way the bait can be retrieved in a natural manner, head first, which often attracts a pike.

Wire traces are essential because of the pike's sharp teeth and these can be made up easily from a length of Alasticum. Ten-pound reel line is quite strong enough for the Severn and is pliable enough to enable control of the tackle while trotting. Stationary dead-baits, so popular on Fenland waters, are used by a few pike specialists on the Severn, usually in winter when the pike are a bit lethargic. These are free-lined in the almost still backwaters and bays, or legered in deep, steady-moving swims.

Spinning and plug fishing is rewarding for smaller pike and it is a good method of covering a lot of water in a short time. There is no necessity for long casting as most pike are found fairly close in. This method can be used in quite shallow water for searching the edges of reed-beds where pike often lie basking in the summer. Brass spoons are very popular on the Severn as they show up well in the peaty-coloured water, but there is plenty of scope for experiment in this field. Timing the strike can be tricky at times when live-baiting, especially in strong currents when it is sometimes difficult to judge whether the pike has stopped its run. Of course, with a multi-hook tackle the strike can be made as soon as the float starts moving, and when spinning there is often no need to strike at all.

Although pike are reputed to give the best sport in winter during the cold weather, Severn pike are active all the year round and good bags are often taken in the summer. What triggers off their feeding mechanism is a mystery, but whatever it is usually brings all the pike in a particular stretch on feed at the same time. When this happens sport can be really hectic for short periods. Autumn, when there is a slight chill in the air, can be very productive providing the river level is right. In this respect a slight lift often brings the pike into a ravenous mood. Probably the best time of all though, is when a sudden rise in air temperature during a prolonged cold spell occurs, due perhaps to a change in wind direction. On such days, when the river is fairly steady and clear, it's a sure bet that pike will be on the prowl. Not that pike are put off by coloured water, on the contrary they will grab a bait when the river is like cocoa. These are the times when, perhaps because they cannot find their natural prey, they often pick up maggots or worms off the bottom.

Roach

There is something about roach that appeals to all anglers, old and young, novice and expert. The bigger samples are probably the most sought after and most admired of all our coarse fish. No matter what other species we may be seeking a nice roach is never unwelcome on the hook. There is nothing more satisfying than to see a dozen or so big 'uns in the keep-net. But what is the reason for their popularity, why do we go out of our way to catch them? They are handsome creatures, it's true. Well proportioned, with bright red fins complementing beautiful but subdued shades of green and blue merging along the top of silvery flanks. Yet, as a quarry, they lack the strength of barbel, the size of bream, the craftiness of chub and the wiliness of dace.

Nevertheless sizeable roach, especially those in popular hard-fished waters, are cunning and shy to a degree that puts them in a class of their own. They ignore all but perfectly presented baits and seem to sense the presence of the smallest hooks. They fight well too, lunging and boring for freedom all the way to the net. I reckon that to tempt and catch 'educated' roach in quantity calls for a culmination of all our angling skills and experience and that, I feel, is the clue to their popularity. When we catch good-class roach, we know we are fishing well and doing everything just right. In this respect the Severn offers ample opportunities to test our prowess.

Although it is not classed as a great roach river, there are considerable numbers present in many areas. At the moment they are overshadowed by barbel, chub and perhaps bream. But they are multiplying quickly following the disease of the 1960s. Already some of the more traditional roach venues such as Shrewsbury, Coalport, Stourport, and Worcester down to Tewkesbury are again producing the kind of catches we took for granted before the species was drastically reduced. The revival didn't begin until 1970 so it will take time for them to become re-established at every venue along the river, but when they do all Severn anglers will rejoice.

Severn roach are not too energetic and though they sometimes appear among the barbel, chub and dace in the fast water, the placid, more gentle swims are much more to their liking. Fortunately there are plenty of such spots on the river and, while roach are perhaps more at home in the even-flowing deeper waters below Stourport, it is surprising how many first-class roach haunts there are in the middle and upper reaches. Bewdley, Arley, Quatford, Knowle Sands, Bridgnorth, Jackfield, Cressage, are all well known barbel and chub stretches, but they also yield a good crop of splendid-quality roach. Above Shrewsbury roach may not be anywhere near so plentiful, but really big ones turn up at many points as far upstream as Newtown and Caersws.

Generally, I suppose you cannot write roach off completely at any venue as, if the character of the river suits them, they soon take up permanent residence. Their main requirement is a reasonable depth of water as their extreme shyness calls for plenty of cover. It is rare to find roach in less than three feet of water except when the river is coloured. On these occasions, they do move into much shallower swims, especially where there is a clean gravel bottom. It is a well-known fact that roach like to feed off a hard gravel or shingle table, and if this isn't available they often settle for a sandy bottom. In fact, when searching for likely roach pitches on a strange venue it is worthwhile studying the ground near the water's edge. If it is gravelly or sandy, there's a good chance that the river-bed is the same and if roach are in the vicinity that is where they will be.

What they don't like is a mud or silt bottom, or any place where rubbish collects, such as backwaters. This is not to say that all backswims are taboo. On the contrary those with a clean bottom are natural havens for roach. Severn roach grow to a good size and fish up to a pound-and-a-half are fairly common on the well-known stretches. Two pounders are hooked occasionally and many above this magic barrier are caught at Shrewsbury. In fact pound roach are the rule rather than the exception along the Quarry and County Ground lengths. Anyone seeking a 'glass case' specimen could do far worse than concentrate on this day-ticket fishery. A recent outstanding catch taken from the Quarry consisted of eleven roach which tipped the scales at 22lb. This magnificent haul was netted on a cold December day by two Cheshire anglers using maggots and breadflake as bait.

A habit of Severn roach which favours anglers is that they like to lie very near the margins. And providing there is an adequate depth, the shoals often move right under the banks where the current is steadier. Of course, it is fatal to generalise and I can recall many days when quality roach have regularly taken large pieces of breadflake trotted down the middle, meant for chub. But this frequently happens on a low clear river along fairly shallow stretches. As a rule, the best time for roach fishing is when there is 'a drop on' and the water is slightly coloured. Fresh water in the river sparks off the roaches' appetites and they become less wary under the screen of colour. These are the days when big catches are made under the rod end, often from swims only 3ft deep.

I have had some wonderful sport in these conditions, but one outing that sticks in my mind was a 'red letter day' at Ironbridge, in summer, when this famous roach venue was at its peak, way back in the 1960s. The river looked a sorry sight, it had risen 18in overnight and, as the popular deep, steady swims were turbulent and 'boiling', I decided to try a ford at the back of the roadside garage. At normal level this particular gravel-bottomed swim is only inches deep, but that day it was a good 2ft and running smoothly, if rather fast. Actually I expected to catch dace, but to my delight liberal offerings of maggots attracted quality roach which fed eagerly. Easing double maggots on a size 16 hook as slowly as possible through the pitch, I caught one after another for two or three hours. I don't know what my total catch amounted to, but I had a job to drag my keep-net from the river. A bailiff who watched me reckoned there was a good half-hundredweight at least and I didn't argue with him. In fact I wasn't too bothered about the weight. More important, I had discovered a good roach pitch when the river was in spate.

Another unforgettable occasion when roach went mad close-in in shallow water (but in winter) was at a fairly recent open contest at Stourport. This time the angler was Birmingham's national team skipper Clive Smith, and he won the match easily with 34lb of prime roach from 3ft of water just beyond his rod tip. That cold day Clive hooked fish after fish up to 1½lb at every cast for a hectic hour as the light was fading. Had he stayed on after the match I am sure he could have doubled his score. An interesting point about this catch, and one that illustrates an important angle about roach, is that although Clive had the shoal in front of him for the whole of the match it wasn't until the light began to fade that the fish came on. Light plays an important part in roach fishing, they don't feed freely in bright conditions. Apart from the times when colour in the river acts as a shield, the best sport is to be had on gloomy overcast days, or at dusk or an hour or two into darkness. Autumn and winter is by far the best time of the year to catch roach during the day.

Probably another reason why roach are so popular is that they will feed freely in the depths of winter. Cold water does not bother them once they have become acclimatised to it though, like other species, it takes a day or two before they become accustomed to a drop in temperature. They don't move around much in these conditions, however, and are usually found in the deepest, slowest-moving swims where they accept almost stationary baits. I have hooked roach when it has been so cold that my rod rings have iced up, and Severn records show that many notable bags have been taken during long freezing spells. On these occasions the governing factor is the water temperature rather than the air temperature, and the nearer it is to 40°F the better the chance of contacting roach.

Maggots have always been a good winter bait for Severn roach but they went out of fashion when casters were introduced about twelve years ago. Now it looks as though they have been 're-discovered' as anglers have suddenly switched to bronze wrigglers. Fashion changes in baits have always intrigued me. I often wonder if a 'new' bait is successful because the fish have tired of or become educated to the more usual offerings, or because previously they never had a chance to show preference. The trouble is that it only needs one angler to catch well with a particular bait and within weeks everyone is using it. It's like a chain reaction. At the moment bronze-coloured maggots are very much in vogue and therefore accounting for most roach hauls.

Yet the chances are that the caster is still equally attractive. Caster is certainly still the number one summer bait, because for some strange reason roach won't look at maggots in warm weather, except maybe the odd fish when the river is in spate. Tares have also made an impact in recent years with many headline catches from lots of venues, mainly in the middle reaches between Bridgnorth and Stourport but also below Worcester and Tewkesbury. This bait is worth experimenting with in any steady fairly deep pitch, as it has attracted huge hauls of roach from several unexpected areas. The Whitmore Reans AA stretch just below Bridgnorth, for instance, was never regarded as a first-class roach venue until tares proved it otherwise. Whether the roach will continue to be caught in such numbers once the novelty of this comparatively new bait wears off remains to be seen, but in the meantime it must be regarded as a top summer roach attractor.

Hempseed too, is taking its toll, which is hardly surprising in view of the huge amounts heaved into the river. Match-anglers use hempseed as groundbait for all species and think nothing of feeding half-a-gallon in a five-hour match, though few try it on the hook. Why should they, when casters or tares—similar but much larger baits and therefore easier to put on the hook—rarely fail? Yet a single grain of hemp will tempt really big roach as Burton-on-Trent angler Roy

Walker has demonstrated several times. He has netted bags of up to 50lb from Bridgnorth, all on hemp.

Before casters and seed baits became popular, roach fishing in summer was considered a waste of time, but I used to have a lot of success with stewed wheat. It wasn't always reliable and often it would take two or three hours of feeding before the roach showed any interest, but when they did the results were well worth it. At one period I became so confident in wheat that I began using it exclusively in club contests and found that it would tempt chub and dace as well as roach. I won two or three matches with it but, as I said, it is a chancy bait and after a few blanks I reverted to the more conventional offerings saving wheat for pleasure outings.

Other popular Severn baits such as luncheon meat, cheese, worms and breadflake account for a lot of roach but usually when anchored with a leger. Breadpaste is useful on the lower reaches especially when float legered. I discovered this while fishing for bream at Ripple, on the Severn-Trent Water Authority stretch. Offering large lumps of paste on a size 10 hook in the hope of some good sample bream, I was troubled with half-hearted bites which I couldn't hit. In desperation I tried smaller pieces and solved the problem. It was roach and not bream nibbling the bait. As soon as I scaled down, the float sailed away every time, and I finished the day with a score or so of roach around the pound mark.

Feeding a roach swim should be done on the 'little and often' principle, depending on how the fish are taking or coming. Loose offerings are preferable whenever possible as roach tend to eat cereal groundbait. But if there is a powerful current or a greater depth, groundbait is essential to get the hook bait samples on the bottom. Medium-ground brown-breadcrumb is ideal and should be mixed so as to be fairly mushy but stiff enough to sink quickly. The best way to ensure it doesn't float is to mix it sloppy at first and then add dry crumb to get the right consistency. When roach are expected many anglers throw in huge quantities of hemp-seed no matter what they are using on the hook. But whether this tactic brings better results is open to conjecture. I can see an advantage perhaps with tares or casters, but not with maggots on the hook.

As I have already remarked, roach are quite cunning and to catch them in numbers, tactics, tackle and bait presentation have to be spot-on. The golden rule is to keep shotting to a minimum with the terminal tackle as fine as possible. For instance, while it is quite likely that roach will take a bait offered on a 1½lb breaking strain hook length, there are times when a more supple 1lb bottom is necessary. The difference is only one-thousandth of an inch but the effect in clear water is sometimes remarkable. The size and weight of the hook is also of paramount importance and besides being matched to the bait it should, whenever possible, be buried out of sight. Roach are often hook-shy which is why small sizes, ie 16, 18 or 20 in fine wire patterns, are popular for casters and maggots. However, for larger baits or when offering double portions, it is sometimes possible to get away with size 14 or size 12.

A peculiarity I have observed about roach in the Severn is that it is often impossible to induce them to move away from their chosen spot in a swim. When they are in this mood no amount of groundbait or feed has any influence. This is not to say that the shoals don't roam around—they do, but only when it suits them. Chub, barbel, dace and bream invariably swim upstream to the source of regular offerings, but not roach. They prefer to lie and wait for the feed to trickle almost into their mouths. I can remember many outings when I have tried everything to attract a shoal upstream where I could catch them with less effort, but to no avail. Having said that I should point out the exception and that seems to be at hard-fished match venues. Here the roach often behave like dace, coming into mid-water to take the bait on the drop.

Generally speaking though, you have to go to the roach, they won't come to you. As most of the best roach swims are located on stretches where the flow is fairly even, sensitive stick or slim balsa floats can be used. Shotted evenly with

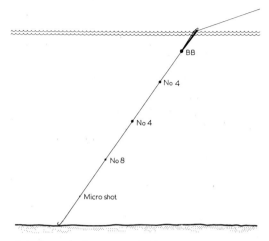

Fig 10 A stick float rig for roach fishing. The shot are evenly spaced

the smallest down towards the hook, the bait will trickle along very temptingly. The size of the float is determined by the depth and force of the current and should carry enough weight to get the bait down to the bottom as quickly as possible. That's where the roach are. They don't rise up in mid-water as often as in other rivers so 'drop bites' are less of a problem. For normal conditions and fishing close in, one BB shot or its equivalent is sufficient weight for every 2ft of depth. The float should be trimmed or cocked until it is a mere dot on the surface so that the most delicate bites can be spotted.

Of course, a perfect tackle set-up is of little use if it is not controlled correctly. Bearing in mind that the surface water always travels at a greater speed than the bottom current, unless a float is held in check it will drag the bait along in an unnatural manner. Also, as I mentioned earlier, roach are often disinclined to chase after food, so the bait should be dragged hard on the bottom slowly. The best way to do this (when conditions allow) is to fish well over-depth and 'inch' the float along by keeping a tight line. After casting slightly upstream, clamp the line with a finger on the spool until the tackle has settled then, by gently lowering the rod and at the same time allowing it to swing round with the flow, the tackle can be eased gently downstream. When the rod arm is fully extended, release enough line to bring the rod back to a vertical position and go through the same motion until you reach the end of the swim. If bites don't come to this method, a good dodge is to hold the float stationary for a few seconds or pull it back slightly. This has the effect of raising the bait off the bottom in an attractive manner and often tempts finicky fish. The same manoeuvre should also be carried out at the end of each run down.

Often when the river is out of sorts or when there is a strong downstream wind, roach simply won't look at a moving bait no matter how slowly it is presented. A popular Severn method on these occasions is to fish close in 'on the strain'. This is a local adaptation of laying on and stretpegging with the bait held stationary at various points in the swim. An Avon or balsa float, carrying a little more lead than usual, is ideal for this method. The shot is placed in a bunch, a foot or so from the hook, and the float pulled up well over-depth so that the weight just rests on bottom.

Another float method, which is useful when the roach are proving difficult, is what I term 'arc-ing' the swim. Simply, it consists of casting a couple of rod lengths out and manipulating the float so that it swings slowly in an arc towards the bank. By gradually casting further downstream the whole of the swim can be covered in this way. The bait is dragged along the bottom and comes to the fish in a different direction, which often induces a bite.

In very bad conditions when float-fishing is impossible, roach can be caught on a light leger or small swimfeeder, but a fast reaction to bites is imperative. The tackle for legering should be rigged to eliminate resistance to bites and fished fairly close in with as much line out of the water as possible. The key to successful legering for roach is fast striking, as bites are short sharp taps with no second chance. While the inexperienced will miss nine out of ten bites, the method can be mastered.

Salmon

Although the Severn can hardly be rated among the country's top salmon rivers it yields a surprising number of fish, both to commercial nets and rod and line each season, as the following table of returns illustrates:

COMMERCIAL NETS BELOW GLOUCESTER

1964—3,115	1969—2,615	1974—3,152
1965—3,660	1970—3,440	1975—3,823
1966—3,195	1971—3,629	1976—2,838
1967—1,968	1972—4,467	1977—1,509
1968—2,061	1973—3,887	

ROD CATCHES—UPPER SEVERN

1964— 48	1969—no	1974— 113
	separate figures	
1965— 59	1970— 50	1975— 192
1966 144	1971— 40	1976— 56
1967— 309	1972 110	1977— 237
1968— 211	1973— 121	

BELOW SHREWSBURY

1964— 248	1969— 332	1974— 401
1965— 243	1970— 248	1975— 850
1966— 573	1971— 447	1976— 403
1967— 930	1972—1,401	1977— 556
1968— 169	1973— 863	

The figures illustrate how the seasonal catches vary considerably from year to year due, in the main, to the average height of the river and weather conditions. Also, it can be seen that until 1977 only a small proportion of the total seasonal figure was taken above Shrewsbury Weir. This situation is now greatly improved since the opening of a new fish pass at the Weir. Most of the salmon caught are

Although better known for its coarse fishing the river also produces fine salmon fishing. This 15-pounder was taken by Vic Jones from the river at Shrewsbury

taken in the spring from the main runs and are a mixture of large and small fish, although in recent years the proportion of grilse has increased remarkably. The majority of salmon are caught below the weirs where they congregate awaiting high water, but a fair amount come from the pools below the many fords upstream of Bewdley. Short, squat and well-marked, Severn salmon do not attain the huge size of those that run up its sister river—the Wye—but they are reputed to be tastier and anglers who fish both rivers reckon they also fight harder.

The Severn salmon season begins on 2 February and one of the most popular spots on opening day is below Diglis Weir at Worcester. This 300-yard stretch, controlled by the Severn-Trent Water Authority, is a prolific salmon pool that yields an average of 300 fish each season, a figure that compares favourably with the top beats on most first-class salmon rivers. Fortunately for salmon enthusiasts it can be fished on day-permits, available to anyone. Another popular salmon fishery is Shrewsbury Weir where the average return is also quite high. Again, this water is open to anyone, but the demand for permits is so great that they have to be drawn from a hat. All the other weir pools are controlled by syndicates or private clubs, although several associations have water in the immediate vicinity of most of them. Salmon pools elsewhere along the river are mostly open to anyone with the appropriate membership card but some associations charge extra for salmon fishing. On the other hand, the Severn-Trent Water Authority has salmon rights on some of its holdings which are available at no extra cost.

The most popular method used on the Severn, especially in weir pools, is spinning devon minnows. Early in the season devons account for nearly all the fish landed, but later on, as the river gets lower and warmer, Mepps and wobblers come into their own. In heavy water, lines need to be strong to combat the powerful currents and many underwater obstructions, but some anglers go as light as 6lb when the river is low and clear. Yellow-bellied devons are good in heavy, coloured water; while silver, black and silver, or gold—in fact any colour of the rainbow (provided that it flashes) seems to catch in clear water. Another good method, particularly for the pools on the middle and upper reaches where long waits for a take call for a lot of patience, is legered lobworms. A bunch of three or four on a size 2 or 4 hook fished in a rolling style through the pools, tempts the salmon. One experienced angler I know actually leaves the bait on the same spot for an hour or more and he manages to land quite a few salmon each season.

While all pools below fords are potential salmon lies they are by no means all productive. In fact, there are many stretches where I have never heard of a salmon being taken. Of course, salmon fishing anywhere other than below the weirs is a very chancy business, it's a matter of being in the right place at the right time. Among the more popular venues are the Raby Estate and the Leighton waters at Cressage. The Prince Albert Angling Society stretch at Atcham contributes to the numbers from the church pool near the bridge; and the Birmingham AA's stretch at Underdale, being quite close to the weir, is rated as the best salmon beat belonging to the Association. Above Shrewsbury Weir, the chances of hooking a salmon have improved enormously since the opening of the new fish pass.

Salmon Details

Season: 2 February to 14 September. Salmon licences are available on a seasonal or daily basis.

Diglis Weir Salmon Fishery: Season-permits are available only to citizens and residents of Worcestershire. These are distributed on the basis of 90 for citizens and ratepayers of Worcester, and 30 for the inhabitants of the old county of Worcestershire. The permits enable the holders to fish every third day i.e. 2, 5, 8, 11 February etc, or 6, 9, 12 February etc. Applications must be received by the first post on 15 November each year. Where the number of applications exceeds the number of permits available, a draw is held at Worcester DUAA HQ. Day-permits cost extra at weekends, and ten-day permits are issued every day throughout the salmon season to non-season permit holders. These are bookable by post from the Severn-Trent Malvern Area Fisheries Office any time up to the fourth working day before the date of fishing. Vacancies thereafter are available to all anglers, season permit holders included.

Applicants are allowed a maximum of eight day-permits in any one month but only four may be for a Saturday or a Sunday. From 1 June onwards, unlimited numbers of permits per applicant are available to all anglers, again season permit holders included. Applications for day-permits for the whole part of the season will be accepted from 1 December. All permits are non-transferable and will not be refunded. Wading, or fishing from boats, is prohibited and a 'spinning only' rule applies until after the end of April. From then on, any legal method may be used providing it doesn't interfere with other anglers. Gaffing is NOT allowed. Only one angler is permitted on each of the clearly marked sections and all anglers must move downstream to the next section every thirty minutes. Between 1 June and 14 September fishing is not allowed before 7 a.m. At all other times fishing will commence one hour before sunrise and cease one hour after sunset. All foul-hooked salmon must be returned.

Shrewsbury Weir—controlled by Shrewsbury & Atcham Council. The Council issues season-permits for residents and non-residents. Residents permits allow fishing on even days of the month, and non-residents fish the odd days until 1 June. Thereafter fishing is allowed on odd and even days. Permits can be obtained, when available, from: The Fisheries Officer, Oakley Manor, Belle Vue Road, Shrewsbury. Fishing is allowed from a point 50yd below the weir to New Park Road, and on all other council-controlled water in the area. Day-permits for non-residents are issued for all water other than below the weir.

Shad

An unusual sporting fish peculiar to the Severn (though they are also found in the Wye) is the shad. Two species, the twaite and the allis, which are migratory members of the herring family, come into the river to spawn in May and early June, the numbers varying from year to year. Twaite are the more common of the two species as the slightly larger allis has become rare in recent years. The shad congregate below the weirs, especially at Tewkesbury, and it is in these areas and below, that they provide excellent sport on small spinners and fly-spoons, as well as other baits and live elvers. In fact, shad enter the river more or less at the same time as elvers.

A net of shad, a herring-like fish which ascends the Severn to spawn. These fish were taken by anglers at Tewkesbury weir

Although they rarely exceed 2lb (the record is only a little over 3lb) they put up the usual frantic fight of a migratory fish which makes them a popular quarry. Hooked on light tackle they don't come easily to the net and many manage to slip the hook. Small bright lures that glitter in the coloured, lashing water as it rushes away from the weirs, attract them like magnets. But they will also grab other baits suspended just off bottom on a float (bear in mind that float-fishing is barred in the close season). Hook size is unimportant but an 8 or 10 will ensure few missed bites.

Catches of as many as 100 shad in a day have been recorded during the main run. Most anglers put them back alive to fight another day, but there are no restrictions on taking them away. Years ago, shad roe was a popular dish and thousands of female fish were slaughtered for the delicacy. Where they go once they have surmounted the lower weirs is a bit of a mystery as few are hooked upstream of Tewkesbury, and I have never heard of any fingerling shad being seen.

Trout

When I first began fishing the River Severn back in the 1950s, it was quite common to hook trout in the shallower stretches as far downstream as Bewdley. In fact, the chances were so good that 'worming' and fly-fishing on the fords along the middle reaches were very popular during the close coarse season. Trout in these areas were never prolific by any means, and we considered ourselves lucky to catch one perhaps at every other outing, but when we did they were invariably good-class fish ranging up to the 3lb mark. Alas, those days are no more. The stocks have declined for various reasons and although 'brownies' are still landed occasionally they are now few and far between.

But thankfully there is still a good head in the upper river which, by its very character, is ideal trout water. Upstream of Newtown, the trout population begins to increase and the further upstream you go the more there are. Indeed, around Llanidloes, the Severn could be described as a typical trout-stream and although it isn't preserved as such, small wild trout thrive in the crystal clear water. Maybe not in such large numbers as we would wish, but in this respect the population is encouraged with an occasional re-stocking by some clubs and associations. At Llandinam, for instance, the Severn-Trent Water Authority obviously have faith in the river's potential as a game river, as they regularly re-stock their Dinam Estate stretch which is classed as a game fishery. This excellent water offers good sport on the fly, both wet and dry, and is available on day- and season-ticket. Several other lengths in the area are also reserved for fly-fishing, especially during the coarse close season. There are long lengths too, where worming and bait fishing is allowed.

I must confess that most of my Severn trout have fallen

for the garden-fly, or lobworm. Although this bait is frowned upon by the purists I have never been averse to using it, particularly when there is extra water in the river. Before I learned to cast a fly, I regarded the worm as the deadliest bait there is for trout, but I learned otherwise one hot June day when the river near Llanidloes was extremely low and gin-clear. After hours of effort I had only one trout to show for my trouble when I noticed an angler fly-fishing. After watching him stalk and hook a fair number of trout, I got into convervation with him and learned some of the secrets of dry fly-fishing. My confidence in the worm diminished somewhat after that experience and it wasn't long before I equipped myself with a fly outfit.

There is no doubt that for low, clear water and calm conditions when the weather is warm, the artificial dry fly takes some beating, especially in the evenings when the trout rise freely. By wading carefully upstream, it is possible to approach an individual rising fish to drop a 'Greenwells Glory' (a good fly on the upper Severn) a few feet above it to float gently downstream almost into its mouth. As long casting is rarely called for, a 9ft rod with no 6 floating line is ideal for the purpose and will cope with most situations. A 3lb cast is a must, however, as although the trout are not big (they average between ½lb and 1lb) it is not unusual to hook a hefty chub.

The middles of pools below fast runs or stickles seem to be the trout's favourite domain, though they can be found in many other types of swim on occasions. Often though, those obvious trout 'rises' turn out to be grayling as the two species inhabit the same type of water. Not that the grayling is any less satisfying on the hook, unless perhaps you happen to be fishing for the pot. Popular dry flies are smallish 'Black and Silvers', 'Williams Favourite', 'Greenwells Glory' and 'Peter Ross'. The latter two patterns along with nymphs etc, are also good for wet fly-fishing across and downstream into the pools early in the season, or in cool weather when there is no natural hatch.

Probably the best months on the upper Severn are April,

May and early June. Fortunately, being the close season for coarse fishing at this time, there is usually plenty of room to roam around searching out the most likely spots. Worming, either upstream or downstream style (when allowed) is a good method early in the season and when the river is carrying extra water. But there is more to this method than merely throwing out a worm and sitting back waiting for results. Trout prefer their food alive, or at least moving, and while they *will* pick up a stationary bait the chances of tempting them are much greater if the bait is trundling downstream towards them. For this method an ordinary long, flat rod can be used, though I prefer a light 8ft spinning rod as this is more gainly in those almost inaccessible areas. A fixed spool reel with 2½lb line loaded to the lip of the spool enables smooth and accurate casting, and a size 10 hook tied direct is about the right size for a nice juicy lobworm. This bait can be 'free-lined' though a single swan shot fastened about a foot from the hook will help casting and also slow the worm's progress in fast water.

When fishing downstream the most important factor is a stealthy approach as trout are extremely shy. The slightest movement is enough to scare them off for an hour or so, so whenever possible it pays to stalk them from behind where they cannot see you. During the coarse season a small buoyant float can be used—a 'Billy Lane Trent Trotter' for instance—to help drag the worm down through the rapids and boulder-strewn lengths into the small pools where the trout invariably lie. This way too a lot of ground can be covered increasing one's chances of finding the trout.

Part 5
Where to Fish

While every care has been taken in compiling details of the listed waters and club secretaries, readers, will appreciate that changes are frequent. Fishery boundaries also are difficult to define accurately, so enquiries should be made before fishing unfamiliar waters. Access points and parking spots are usually listed on club membership cards and should be adhered to rigidly as violation leads to loss of waters.

Llanidloes to Caersws

Above Llanidloes the river is little more than a narrow, very shallow trout-stream, though there are deeper pools below the fast runs where the current cascades over huge boulders and slabs of rock. Because of the acidity of this mountain-water the trout, which form the bulk of the fish population, are quite small and rarely exceed half-a-pound. However, being extremely wild and shy they fight like demons, and good sport can be had on the fly as well as with worms (where it is allowed). The Birmingham AA stretch on this length is strictly fly only during the trout season, but Llanidloes AC allow bait fishing on their water.

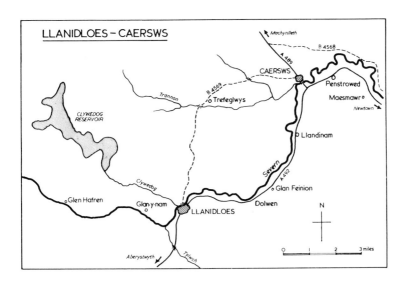

Below the town, and bolstered by the influx of the River Clywedog, the Severn begins to widen as it races through gravel beds and rocky channels, and coarse fish begin to

133

show in numbers. There are plenty of dace, chub and grayling as well as trout in this area. The dace grow big, and fish up to 12oz are quite common. Generally speaking, the upper river fishes best when there is fresh water in, but even then it is gin-clear and special care is needed not to alarm the fish. Mobility is the keyword for success as the shoals easily take fright in the shallow water.

While light float tactics with maggot or casters catch the dace, grayling and smaller chub, good sport can be had by stalking the solitary big chub which haunt the more inaccessible spots. Live minnows, trotted through the pools and under the banks often tempt these predatory monsters in summer, while legered worms, bread, or cheese attract them in autumn and winter. Sport on the fly is excellent for trout and grayling and one notable fishery is the Severn-Trent Water Authority stretch at Llandinam which is regularly stocked with trout though they are on the small side.

Llanidloes AC control a lengthy stretch of the left bank above the town, and both banks downstream of the town bridge as far as Red Bridge. Season- and day-permits are available from Mr Owen, Chemist, Llanidloes, Powys. The Birmingham AA have a long piece of the left bank above the town which is restricted to fly only during the trout season. The fishery starts a little way below Glen Hafren Bridge and extends for ¾ mile downstream.

Warrington AA control the right bank starting below the town to Dolwen Bridge and the left bank from below the bridge. No day-permits are issued but membership is open to anyone through the secretary. At Upper Penrhyllan, a mile of right bank is available on day-permits from Mr S. Price, Upper Penrhyllan, Dolwen, near Llanidloes, Powys.

Downstream at Llandinam, the Severn-Trent Water Authority control 4½ miles of both banks which is available on day- and season-permits. The fishery is divided into coarse and game, and separate permits are issued for each. The game fishery extends from Llandinam to the Trannon confluence, and the coarse fishery from the Trannon confluence to the upper boundary of Caersws Recreation Ground, plus one meadow of the right bank below Caersws Bridge. Grayling fishing (fly only) is also permitted on the game fishery during the coarse season. Permits are available from **Mr** Evan Jones, 2 Broneiron Cottages, Llandinam, Powys.

Caersws to Newtown

Similar to the river upstream but less rugged, this reach is a little deeper and wider in parts. Because of a long series of loops and turns the current is also somewhat slower. While the trout population gradually thins out as the river moves towards Newtown, there is a good stock of coarse fish but it is patchily distributed. Chub, dace and grayling, with a few pike, make up the numbers. Salmon are an attraction on this length and a notable beat is the Birmingham AA's Red House fishery which contains several good holding pools. Some of the biggest grayling in the Severn are found towards Newtown and the best bait to attract them is casters.

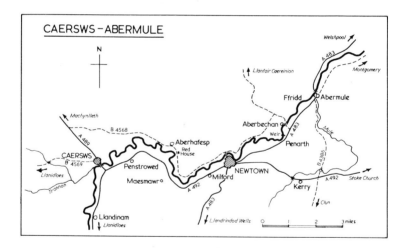

The Birmingham AA owns the rights on the left bank beginning at the end of the first meadow below Caersws road bridge and extending downstream for $\frac{3}{4}$ mile to the hospital. The association also control a mile of the right bank beginning at the boundary of the Severn-Trent Water Authority stretch below the bridge. Maesmawr Hall Hotel owns a mile stretch in this area on the right bank adjacent to the hotel and permits are available. Day-ticket water is also available at nearby Dolhafren Farm which controls ¾ mile of right bank and tickets can be obtained from Mr Williams. At Red House, the BAA lease both banks for ¾ mile.

Below here, at Tymawr Farm, Warrington AA has the rights on both banks, and Montgomeryshire AA have the right bank at Penstrowed. This Association, which incorporates three local angling clubs, controls several stretches of the river, permits for which are available as follows: Full county permit for county residents; outside county, full-permit and weekly-permits. Further details from the secretary. Also at Penstrowed, adjoining the MAA water, is one meadow belonging to Crewe Amalgamated AA. This association lease several lengths downstream, and though no day-tickets are issued, membership is open to anyone through the secretary. Montgomery AA lease another left bank stretch from the derelict weir at Milford downstream to Newtown laundry. On the right bank the BAA have ½ a mile, just above Mochdre Brook, and a few meadows below the brook the Severn-Trent Water Authority own a lengthy stretch which extends into Newtown.

Newtown to Welshpool

(See also map page 136)

Still widening and with varying depths up to 8ft, the river supports plenty of chub in this area. In fact, they are the dominant species. The shoals are nowhere as large as those found on the middle and lower reaches but the fish attain a good size. Four-pounders are fairly common while five-pounders turn up occasionally. Tactics to catch them vary and though it is possible to build up respectable catches with a float in the straight, deeper swims, the leger is often the best method in the pools below fords. Salmon are caught regularly all along this length but the most noted spot is below Aberbechan Weir. Plenty of pike are taken around

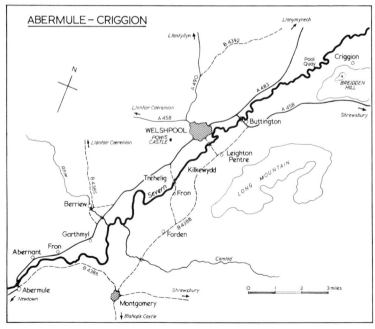

Abermule and dace and grayling turn up almost everywhere. Roach begin to figure in catches from Newtown downstream but the shoals are generally small and not too easy to locate.

Montgomeryshire AA and the Severn-Trent Authority control most of the river through the town—details of boundaries from Mr L. Bebb, Tackle Shop, Newtown, Powys. Below the town, Crewe Pioneers have $\frac{3}{4}$ mile piece of left bank. No day-tickets are issued but membership is open to anyone through the secretary. Crewe Amalgamated lease the adjoining left bank stretch and immediately below this, The White Swan Piscatorials have four meadows. The Severn-Trent Water Authority then have another stretch (free to Severn licence holders) which extends to Penarth Weir.

The right bank below the Severn-Trent water is private for about $1\frac{1}{2}$ miles and then Crewe Pioneers have another short length. Adjoining this is Prince Albert AS water. This club controls many miles of the river as far downstream as Shrewsbury. No day-tickets are issued and there is a waiting-list to join—details of membership from the secretary. The right bank from here on is privately controlled to below Aberbechan Bridge. At Aberbechan the Birmingham AA have a left bank stretch which extends above and below the Bridge. Crewe Pioneers then have $\frac{3}{4}$ mile which adjoins the BAA water. On the right bank, Montgomeryshire AA water starts at the meadow directly behind Tanyffordd and continues downstream to the confluence of the River Mule. The Association also lease the left bank above and below the road bridge at Abermule. Both banks are private from here to Abernant where Crewe Pioneers have one mile of the right bank. Adjoining the Pioneers stretch is a length owned by Warrington AA, known as Caerhowell Hall. Day-ticket water in this area is available from the Lion Hotel, Caerhowell, who have a $\frac{1}{4}$ mile of left bank, and Mr G. Watkins, Red House Farm, Halfway, Montgomeryshire, who controls $1\frac{1}{4}$ miles of the right bank.

Downstream the left bank is privately controlled as far as Lugg Brook, then Crewe Pioneers have a further $2\frac{1}{2}$ miles

The author wades a shallow ford at Leighton on the upper reaches of the river above Welshpool

of right bank at Garthmyl. At Forden, Cheshire AA lease 2 miles of right bank from the confluence of the Camlad to the boundary of the BAA water. The BAA length extends for 2 miles to just above Kilkewydd Bridge. On the left bank Crewe Pioneers have the stretch immediately below Lugg Brook, and this extends to Prince Albert AS water at Trehelig. Crewe Amalgamated AA then take over the left bank as far as Kilkewydd Bridge.

Below Kilkewydd the Severn-Trent Water Authority lease both banks as well as a short stretch of the left bank above the bridge. This is free fishing to licence holders. At the downstream left boundary of the Severn-Trent water, Crewe Amalgamated take over as far as Lower Leighton Bridge. They also have the right bank stretch upstream of the bridge. The left bank, downstream of Leighton Bridge belongs to Montgomeryshire AA, and extends to the old weir. Liverpool AA have 2 miles of the right bank between Leighton and Buttington. No day-permits are issued but membership is open through the secretary. At Welshpool, Crewe Pioneers have a further 1 mile of left bank, and Hazeldine AA have a short length in this area for members only.

140

Welshpool to Shrewsbury

(See also map page 138)

Although the river is quite narrow in places as it leaves Welshpool, it has broadened to almost middle reach-proportions by the time it arrives at Shrewsbury. It is quite deep in places too. The fishing along this length is very patchy, however, and though quite hefty bags of chub are taken at odd venues it is recognised as one of the poorest parts of the river. Chub are the dominant species in all areas, though good-class roach and dace also figure in catches. Odd barbel are caught now and again, and no doubt it won't be very long before these fish are as well-established as they are below Shrewsbury. Pike are taken at most points, but the Montford Bridge district is perhaps the most noted venue for this species. Many fish over 20lb have been caught from the river downstream of the bridge. The dace and roach fishing used to be excellent in the Montford Bridge area but sadly these species have declined alarmingly in recent years.

The Birmingham AA have holdings on both banks above the railway bridge at Buttington, while Crewe Amalgamated have water between the railway and road bridges, also on both banks. Further downstream, the BAA have another mile or so of left bank on each side of Maginnis Bridge. In the Pool Quay area, there are extensive BAA holdings on both banks. The left bank stretch starts at Maesydd, and extends for $1\frac{1}{4}$ miles, and after a short break continues on to Pool Quay.

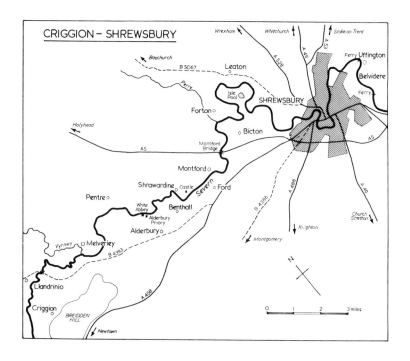

The right bank section starts opposite Foel Coppice and extends downstream for 2 miles towards Criggion. Crewe Pioneers have a lengthy stretch at Trewerne extending for 4½ miles along the right bank. Cheshire AA lease the Red House Farm water at Ardleen which is a one-mile length of the left bank. At Llandrinio, the BAA have the right bank above and below the bridge, and Cheshire AA have the opposite bank.

Prince Albert AS control 1½ miles of left bank downstream at the Haim, and a further mile at Haimwood. More BAA water follows on the right bank with ¾ mile at Acre Lane, and ½ mile at Crew Green. Prince Albert AS lease two meadows on the right bank at Crew Green and ¾ mile of left bank at Newbridge. At Melverley, the Tontine Hotel has a small stretch available for contests, and the Severn-Trent Water Authority control a stretch of left bank below the confluence of the River Vyrnwy—free fishing to licence holders.

142

Downstream at Alberbury, Crewe Pioneers lease $3\frac{1}{2}$ miles of right bank and $\frac{3}{4}$ mile of left bank, and the BAA have a further $1\frac{1}{2}$ miles of right bank. The Cheshire AA take over one meadow on the left bank at Pentre; and at Royal Hill, Prince Albert AS have $\frac{3}{4}$ mile of left bank—day-ticket water is available in this area from the Royal Hill Inn, Edgerley, Oswestry, Salop. At Ford, Crewe Pioneers control $\frac{3}{4}$ mile of the right bank. More day-ticket water is available at the Ferry Farm, Shrawardine, and at Perry Heath Farm, Mytton, near Montford Bridge. The Wingfield Arms has day-ticket water on the right bank immediately above the bridge, and Crewe Pioneers have $\frac{1}{2}$ mile of left bank while the BAA lease $\frac{1}{4}$ mile of left bank immediately below the bridge. Sabrina AC lease 6 miles of the left bank below the confluence of the River Perry, and membership for this club is open through the secretary. Whitmore Reans AA have a stretch on the right bank which is available to members only. Adjoining this water is the BAA Bicton fishery which extends for $\frac{3}{4}$ mile to where Prince Albert AS once more take over for 5 miles downstream.

Anglers fishing the Quarry waters near the centre of Shrewsbury, a popular summer and winter venue

Shrewsbury to Atcham

Shrewsbury is the place to go for specimen roach and chub, though large bags of smaller fish are also taken. Big barbel are not uncommon, while below the town bream often figure in catches from the steadier swims. But the Severn hereabouts is notoriously fickle and sometimes defeats the most expert anglers even when it looks perfect. Shrewsbury Weir, almost in the centre of the town, is a dividing line in the character and sport potential of the river which forms a loop before it rushes towards Atcham. Above the Weir, the Severn is steady-flowing with plenty of really deep stretches —it runs up to 14ft in parts. This more placid water fishes best from autumn onwards when the boats and crowds have gone, but good bags are sometimes recorded in summer especially by mid-week anglers.

Tares, combined with hempseed, have proved a deadly bait for roach in recent years, so too have bronze-coloured maggots. Probably the most popular stretches are the Quarry and County Ground lengths which lie on opposite banks above and below the Welsh Bridge. Roach are likely to turn up at most pegs at the bottom end of the County Ground and in the middle of the Quarry length, usually in swims over 5ft deep. One of the best areas lies in front of a statue of Hercules opposite the boathouse, and it was here that Ron Baker landed a superb 74½lb haul of chub. The bend on the County Ground opposite the roadside garage is a noted big-chub haunt, which has produced large catches and specimens to over 5lb.

Below the Weir, the Severn is a completely different river which races through fords, glides and gullies, steadying and deepening occasionally at Underdale, Emstrey and Uffington until it widens and shallows above Atcham Bridge. Barbel, chub and dace give good sport around the fords while bream and roach often figure in catches from the deeper pitches. The Emstrey length is famous for its bream which run up to 6lb in weight. Many hauls approaching 100lb have been made here, usually to breadflake or worms.

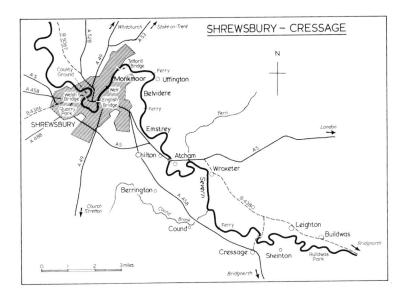

Shrewsbury Corporation issue day-tickets and season-permits through tackle shops and patrolling bailiffs for many miles of river above, in, and below the town. On the right bank water is available at Doctors Fields, the County Ground, Burrsfield, the back of the Gay Meadow and down to the railway bridge. There are nine meadows of right bank fishing at Monkmoor, four below the lane being reserved for individual anglers. Fishing on the left bank starts at Coton Hill and runs down through the Quarry to below the Weir. The Monkmoor fishery, and the water below the Weir, is closed to coarse fishing between 2 February and 16 June to give the salmon anglers a chance. The Quarry, County Ground and part of Moonkmoor can be booked for contests through Mr Sid Peters, 37 York Road, Shrewsbury, Salop. Free fishing is allowed from the towpaths along the river

A picturesque scene on the river at Pimley, near Shrewsbury

on the right bank below the Welsh Bridge and on the left bank below English Bridge.

Above the town from Berwick to Shelton, the Shrewsbury AS and the Shifnal AC control $3\frac{1}{2}$ miles of the left bank. Membership is open (including salmon) to anyone but day-permits are not issued. Contests are allowed, however, and details can be obtained from Mr G. Howells, 4 Coppice Road, Shifnal, Salop. Shropshire Anglers' Federation also have a piece nearby Berwick, and again while this is for affiliated members it can be booked for contests through Mr Bill Ball, 9 The Grove, Hadley, Telford, Salop. Ditherington AC, a local club, lease many miles of the river below the Weir. Membership is open and full cards or weekly permits are issued by local tackle suppliers. Match bookings are accepted through Mr J. Almond, 35 Sundorn Crescent, Shrewsbury, Salop. Rolls-Royce AC have a stretch not far down from the Weir, this is members-only but contests of 50 to 60 pegs are permitted. Details from Mr D. Flower, 1 Windermere Road, Shrewsbury, Salop.

The Shrewsbury Old Sports LMS AC have a lengthy stretch at Emstrey; permits, details and match-booking from Mr John Thorpe, 13 Hordley Avenue, Heath Farm, Shrewsbury or tackle supplier H. W. Phillips, 9 Abbey Foregate, Shrewsbury, Salop. St Helens Ramblers AC control $1\frac{1}{2}$ miles of right bank just above the town and a piece below Belvedere Bridge. This is members-only water—details from Mr J. Prestcott, 76 Birchley Street, St Helens, Lancs. At Underdale, the Birmingham AA have a lengthy piece of the right bank, which lies each side of Telford Bridge. Salmon rights are included but the water is frequently booked for contests at weekends. Prince Albert AS have several small stretches in this area including salmon fishing, but this is strictly reserved for members.

Upstream of Atcham Bridge, on the left bank, is the Severn-Trent Water Authority's Paradise Meadows which is available to any Severn licence holder. The Authority also control the coarse fishing on the opposite bank for approximately $\frac{1}{2}$ mile, though Prince Albert AS hold the salmon rights. This roadside stretch is fairly deep where the current runs near the bank.

Atcham to Cressage

(See map page 145)

From Atcham Bridge to Cressage the river meanders, widens and narrows, through a series of fords, long featureless straights and deep pools, a length that offers a wide choice of methods and tactics. Barbel, chub and dace are the main species though odd shoals of roach are beginning to make an impact here and there. Pike are plentiful in the steadier waters and a few trout are taken off the fords. This span of the river has been very patchy for a number of years, though an improvement in parts has become noticeable in recent seasons. Because of its mainly shallow depth, the best fishing is had in the summer with chub feeding best in winter.

The Atcham area is noted for its big barbel, especially below the mouth of the River Tern which runs in on the left bank above Wroxeter. The long, straight piece downstream of the confluence has yielded many fish up to 8lb, and I hear numerous tales of monsters that got away. Spectacular hauls of smaller barbel, approaching the 100lb mark, were made in 1973 and 1974, but the shoals have thinned out since then as few bonanza catches have been reported recently. This particular part of the river is famous for having produced several Birmingham AA Annual winning catches over the past few years—all barbel. Around Wroxeter Island, chub predominate and anyone prepared to make the long walk will find breadflake, trotted down the middle, very rewarding.

A noted 'hot spot' on the left bank is the ford where a brook enters the river in the middle of the Provincial AA waters below the Tern. This area has yielded huge bags of dace, chub and barbel and regularly produces winning contest catches. From Berrington downstream, the river

148

follows a fairly straight course but the character continues to vary considerably in places. At Cound Lodge, for instance, it forms a big deep pool (above the Hotel) which is noted for pike. And immediately below, the river races through a narrow gulley that has accounted for some of the biggest catches of barbel ever taken from the Severn. This is the spot where I watched Ron Baker land a hundred-weight of fish up to 7lb, all hooked on float-fished casters.

The Severn-Trent Water Authority control the right bank downstream from Atcham Bridge for $3\frac{1}{2}$ miles. This is free fishing for licence holders. The fishing is divided into numbered meadows, six of which are strictly reserved for individual anglers. The remainder is heavily match-fished at weekends. Access for the downstream end involves a very long walk unless permission is obtained to use the Brompton car park. Club fishing contests here should contact Severn-Trent fishery inspector, Mr G. Williams, 14 Allerton Road, Harlescott, Shrewsbury, Salop, for a permit to park at the farm.

Birmingham AA's Berrington fishery starts at the downstream boundary of the Authority stretch, just below Wroxeter Island, and continues to a private meadow above Cound Brook. Birmingham AA water begins again at the mouth of the Brook and runs for a further mile to the Cound Lodge Hotel. The water immediately behind the Hotel belongs to Ansells Brewery and is reserved for guests. The right bank below the Hotel is private until the start of the Raby Estate fishery which continues to Cressage Bridge. The Estate waters can be fished on a day- or season-permit available on the river bank from patrolling bailiffs or from, the Estate Office, Uppington, Telford, Salop. Match bookings are also available.

The left bank immediately below Atcham Bridge is controlled by the Mytton and Mermaid Hotel and reserved for guests. The adjoining meadow belongs to the church and occasional permits are issued. Prince Albert AS then take over for 2 miles. Provincial AA water begins at the Prince Albert boundary above Tern mouth and, apart from a short break, continues to Wroxeter. Membership of the PAA is through affiliated clubs but honorary cards can be obtained from the secretary. Except for a short private length the remainder of the left bank as far as Cressage belongs to the Raby Estate which offers similar facilities as for the right bank.

Cressage to Bridgnorth

There is little change in the river below Cressage as it continues to meander, running swiftly across fords, steadying and deepening into pools, and then racing away again through Leighton and Buildwas and down into the Ironbridge Gorge. The species too remain the same in this district, though they are spread out a little more evenly than in the section above. The Leighton area is famous for its big barbel, and a 12½lb monster was landed from just above the well-known S-bend at the bottom of Leighton Bank. (Unfortunately, it was hooked out of season by a salmon angler and never received the publicity it deserved.) Chub are found in most swims along this reach, especially around the fords, but also

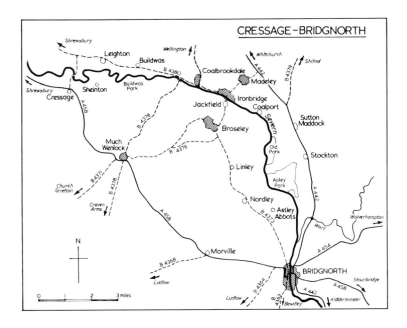

CRESSAGE – BRIDGNORTH

151

in the slower water. Dace are on the increase and, according to reports, roach too are coming back strongly. In fact, catches of 2oz roach are now becoming a regular feature, a sure sign that there has been some successful spawning in recent years.

Once past the ford, downstream of Buildwas Bridge, the river deepens and slows its pace quite suddenly as it cuts through the Gorge. The stretch below the power station runs up to 12ft deep and in its heyday was probably the best roach fishery on the river. Alas, it fell victim to the roach disease and has only lately begun to show signs of recovery. Barbel are present in fair numbers, however, indeed the outflow from the power station—one of two on the river—was one of the first established barbel pitches on the Severn. Probably because of the warm water discharges, it yields good catches even in winter when the river is high and coloured.

Downstream of the old Iron Bridge, the river remains quite deep but it narrows considerably as it forces its way through giant boulders and rocks. This is a very turbulent span of water with rugged banks. It is difficult to fish because of the uneven, snaggy bottom. Below the spinney, on the right bank, the river widens again and then gradually shallows into rapids and pools to well below the Free Bridge. The rapids are full of chub and dace plus barbel which provide excellent sport in summer and occasionally in winter.

Now the river steadies again for a short while before speeding away again into another irregular series of fords, guides and deep pools at Coalport. This is an excellent stretch of water that yields plenty of roach in places as well as the usual chub, dace and barbel. Tares, which caught on well in this area, produced bags of roach up to 50lb during the hot summers of 1975 and 1976. On now, towards Bridgnorth, past Linley suspension bridge and the Apley Estate where the river is quite deep in places but the inevitable shallows predominate. Occasionally huge outcrops of sandstone rock create narrow gullies and channels which are full of chub and barbel in the summer.

A stretch of the river at Linley, near Bridgnorth. Vast shoals of chub and barbel are present providing excellent summer and autumn fishing

Below Linley some of the most outstanding hauls of chub and barbel ever caught from the river have been taken. One particular length is appropriately called 'barbel alley' by the locals, an apt name too, judging by the catches it yields. Regretfully, it is on private club water and the only time visitors get a crack at the shoals is during a few open contests. There are lots of big pike hooked along this reach throughout the season, and huge bream also figure in catches at times. Trout are not uncommon, and many good perch are starting to show.

Leighton Salmon and Coarse Fishing Club control about five miles of both banks as far downstream as Buildwas.

Membership is limited and no permits are issued. Coventry DAA have one huge meadow on the right bank in the middle of the Leighton waters. This is for members only too, and applications for membership should be made via the respective secretaries. The Birmingham AA Buildwas fishery, which includes both banks, adjoins the Leighton waters and continues downstream for 1½ miles as far as a piece of CEGB water just above Buildwas Bridge.

A short distance below the Bridge, on the left bank, the BAA have another ¼ mile. Shifnal AC lease the meadow in between the bridge and the BAA waters which run downstream as far as the power station bridge. Below here begin the Ironbridge AC waters which, except for three short breaks, continue downstream along the left bank as far as the Wharfage in the town. This is day-ticket water and permits are issued by local bailiffs on the river-bank. Ironbridge AC also have a short stretch of left bank below the Iron Bridge. Contests are allowed through the secretary. The CEGB control the right bank below Buildwas Bridge as far as the power station, where Dawley AC then take over a long span which runs on to the Free Bridge below Ironbridge. Dawley AC issue day-tickets via patrolling bailiffs and contest bookings are allowed through the secretary.

The left bank above and below the Free Bridge belongs to The Queen's Arms which issues day-tickets. Then, in between two short stretches leased by Telford AA, is free Severn-Trent water. The Brewery Inn has a day-permit length at Coalport where tickets are issued on the bank by a bailiff. Apart from another short Telford AA piece, the remainder of the left bank is private as far as the Apley Estate boundary. Telford AA control several short lengths of the right bank below the Free Bridge, and then the Rowley Regis AC take over for 3 miles as far as Linley. No permits are issued by this club.

The Apley Estate own both banks from below Coalport to Bridgnorth. The right bank is leased to two Bridgnorth clubs, the Comrades, and the Bridgnorth AS. Permits are not available for this water and membership of the clubs is

154

restricted to local residents. A few permits are issued for the left bank as far as Winscote through the Apley Estate Office, Bridgnorth, Salop. Another local club, the Bridgnorth British Legion, then take over from the Worfe confluence to the 'milk factory'. A limited number of permits are available through the club secretary. Kinver Freeliners AC lease a small length near the milk factory, then the Bridgnorth British Legion take over the remaining bank as far downstream as the café meadow above Bridgnorth Bridge. The water in front of the café is private but there is some free fishing immediately above and below the Bridge on both banks.

Bridgnorth to Hampton Loade

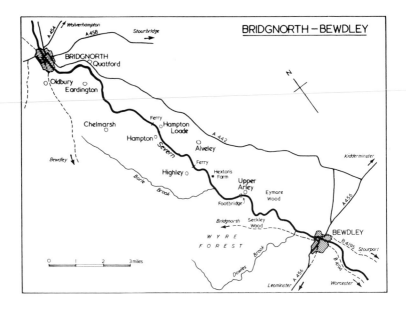

Set in magnificent scenery, with the Severn Valley Railway running alongside, this wonderful stretch is, without doubt, the most popular and heavily fished part of the river. Together with the Arley to Bewdley reach, it is a mecca for Midland anglers as well as many holidaymakers from all over the country. The banks, which are often quite steep, are crowded every day in the summer and at weekends in the winter, and the well-known 'hot spots' are rarely unoccupied. Yet, despite this intense fishing, sport is often excellent as the fords, glides and pools, and the long steady runs are absolutely full of fish.

When the river is right, huge catches of barbel and chub are a regular occurrence everywhere, while roach and dace

156

also figure in bulging keep-nets. Odd big bream, pike, trout and occasional salmon add to the excitement. The full potential of this water is seen when top match anglers gather for one of the popular Birmingham AA Welfare contests in the summer. At these events, 40lb bags usually fail to make the prize-list, and at the 1976 BAA Team Championships the six-man squad representing Coleshill AA totalled an incredible 220lb. Barbel usually form the bulk of these mammoth hauls, but chub also figure quite considerably. In fact, the two species often inhabit the same swims.

A particularly pleasing feature of this length over the past few years has been the re-appearance of roach. Large bags are taken from the steadier swims either with tares or casters in the summer and autumn, or maggots in the winter. Finding the roach swims is not too difficult as they are invariably in steady water with a depth of 5ft or more. There are plenty of such pitches scattered along both banks but especially outstanding is the middle section of the Whitmore Reans AA stretch, the top of the Birmingham AA's Danery water, and parts of Knowle Sands and Quatford. Successful tactics are a lightly shotted stick float fished reasonably close in, supporting single casters, tares or even a grain of hempseed. But, while roach perhaps appeal more to the experts, it is the barbel that draw the crowds.

It may sound an exaggeration but barbel can be caught anywhere along this part of the river. Of course, some pitches are better than others and some are quite outstanding. Probably the best-known barbel pitches are two on the BAA's Quatford stretch. The first is at the top of the trees below the café access track, and the other is opposite Hay Brook—half-an-hour's walk downstream. These two pitches must have yielded tons of barbel over the past few years and they are always occupied. Other noted barbel swims are on the fords along the Whitmore Reans AA water, opposite the 'stack' at Eardington, above Hampton Loade spinney, and the downstream end of the spinney. There are also several good pegs near the pumphouse between the spinney and the ferry. The top method is undoubtedly the swimfeeder either with maggots or casters but many fish also fall to float tactics and legered luncheon meat.

Chub are not quite as prolific as barbel but there is a large head spread in more localised spots. These areas are usually where the banks are tree-lined, in the fast-flowing or the deeper, steady lengths. Some of the best chub swims are found in the middle of the Whitmore Reans water where fine and far-off float tactics, either with casters or breadflake, account for big catches. Chub can be caught very close in on some parts of the stretch, however, such as the top of Knowle Sands where the main current sweeps down the margin of the right bank. There are many more excellent chub swims in the middle of Knowle Sands and Quatford, and the Brook section.

Virtually every meadow of this stretch is open to anyone with the appropriate association membership card. Free fishing is allowed for a few hundred yards on each side of Bridgnorth Bridge, then on the left bank is a short Birmingham AA length reserved for individuals. Following the next two meadows, which are private, is the Whitmore Reans AA water which extends for 1 mile. This can be fished

The river at Knowle Sands

Fred Bailey, one of the best-known and most successful of Severn anglers, lands a chub from a swim at Quatford

on day-tickets but permits must be obtained in advance through the secretary. Access is difficult but, for a fee payable to the caretaker, it is possible to approach through Furness's caravan-site which lies off the Bridgnorth-Kidderminster Road.

The BAA's Danery waters adjoin the Whitmore Reans boundary and continue to the end short meadow which belongs to Kinver Freeliners. The following short pieces above and below the rock are private. Birmingham AA water starts again below the café at Quatford and extends to Hampton Loade Ferry. On the right bank, the free water below Bridgnorth Bridge extends to the back of the garage and then follows a short private length adjoined by Coventry

DAA water. The next major stretch is the BAA's Knowle Sands fishery which starts at the caravan-site below the Coventry piece and, apart from two short gaps at Eardington spinney and just above Hay Brook, extends to the Unicorn Inn at Hampton Loade. The Inn controls two meadows above the Ferry which can be fished on day-tickets.

Hampton Loade to Bewdley

(See map page 156)

From Hampton Loade Ferry down to Bewdley the river is quite rugged in places. Boulder-strewn rocky channels and sandstone outcrops force the currents from one bank to another though there are several long, steady straights separating the interminable fords, broken shallows and glides. Fishing along this stretch can be a little patchy, especially in the Arley area, though huge catches of chub, barbel and roach as well as dace occasionally hit the headlines. The river around Pitt's Island, for instance, supports a vast head of chub, many of them quite big by Severn standards.

Barbel too, are equally thickly spread in this area. Big ones, around the 8lb mark, have been landed between Pitt's Island and the Colliery Bridge. One of the best barbel haunts at Arley is the shallow length of the left bank opposite the old farmhouse above the confluence of Borle Brook. Some remarkable catches have been made here, both in matches and by pleasure anglers. Chub are more dominant below this spot but it is good to note that roach and dace are on the increase. Below Arley some of the biggest chub landed from the Severn in recent years, 7lb plus fish, are reputed to have come from the Sheldon Heath club day-ticket water.

The river now sweeps past Seckley Wood and on through a series of sandstone-slabbed fords which mark the beginning of the Kidderminster DAA Hawkesbatch water. The right bank stretch is one of the best mixed fisheries along the river. Chub, barbel, roach and dace are thickly spread in the fast, shallow water, and catches both in contests and by individual anglers are regularly recorded. The Brideswell fords are particularly outstanding in summer and autumn,

The Severn at Hampton Loade, a popular venue for Severn anglers

while the steady deeper stretches above and below the confluence of Dowles Brook sometimes excel in cold weather. One of the most famous pitches in this area is marked by the old 'gas works' building. Here barbel catches often dominate contests week after week, and pleasure anglers have been known to fill two keep-nets during a day's session. It was this pitch that yielded up the Severn match catch-record of 114lb in August 1978. The angler, Les Taylor from Cradley Heath, West Midlands, caught all barbel up to 3lb with swimfeeder tackle.

On the left bank, from the Lion Inn below the Ferry, is Pitt's waters. Permits are available from Lye Hall or on the bankside. This stretch extends to Pitt's Island and permits can be obtained from Mr M. Storey, Fishing Tackle, Sutton Road, Kidderminster, and Mr A. Hooper, Post Office Stores, Stourton. Below Colliery Bridge is Birmingham AA water which continues to below the footbridge at Arley. Adjoining the BAA water at Trimpley is a day-ticket stretch controlled by Sheldon Heath Social Club Limited, 26 Brays Road, Sheldon, Birmingham. Tickets for this length obtained in advance cost much less than on the bankside.

The next open water is a small day-ticket meadow half-a-mile above Bewdley Bridge. The BAA also have a very short stretch in this area and below this there is some free fishing as far as the Bridge. On the right bank, BAA water begins immediately below the ferry and continues to the Ship Inn at Highley. The Ship Inn owns two meadows for which day-tickets are issued. Birmingham AA waters then continue for 2½ miles to just above Arley footbridge. The Harbour Inn waters, consisting of three meadows, adjoin the BAA stretch and these can be fished on day-permits available on the river-bank.

Below the Harbour Inn water, is a two-meadow stretch belonging to Unity House Farm, Arley (tickets available). Bewdley AS lease the next length which fronts Seckley Wood. Limited subscriptions through the secretary. The next three meadows, which extend to just below the waterworks bridge, belong to The White Swan Piscatorials, a club which controls several more lengths of the river. Membership may be obtained through the secretary but it is strictly limited and there is a waiting list to join. Kidderminster DAA waters follow and continue as far as the Severn-Trent storm-pipe at Dog Lane above Bewdley Bridge. Full members (application through secretary) must belong to an affiliated club within a 15 mile radius of the town, but honorary cards can be purchased from local tackle dealers. From Dog Lane to Bewdley is free water.

Bewdley to Stourport

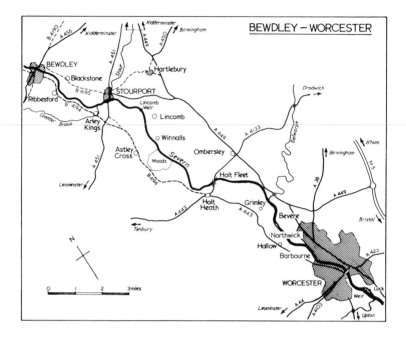

Still quite shallow but steady as it leaves Bewdley, the river races through Lax Ford before deepening slightly on the run into Winterdyne. Shallowing again but with deeper pools, channels and gullies around an island, it sweeps past Blackstone Rock, a huge landmark towering above the last ford on the river. Steadying again, and running quite deep in places (up to 14ft) the Severn now begins to flow evenly and more stately as it approaches Stourport. Depths around here vary between 5ft and 10ft. Although much of the left bank is private, this stretch is one of the most popular and hardest fished lengths of the river. The two towns are holiday and weekend resorts which attract anglers from all

166

over the country, and they come back time and time again as the fishing is first-class.

Chub, dace and roach are spread in all areas with plenty of barbel here and there, not to mention a huge shoal of bream at Ribbesford. While the chub, dace and roach can be found in almost every pitch, the barbel thin out somewhat below Blackstone. Above the rock, large shoals haunt the Winterdyne area. The free water, just below Bewdley Bridge, also produces many big catches early in the season. One of the most noted barbel pitches along the length is the gully between the island in the middle of Winterdyne. Some huge catches have been made here and it is always a favourite contest peg. Towards Stourport, barbel are more localised but there are some really big shoals that invariably produce hefty contest catches. One of the best-known is 'the stones' area halfway along the Lyttleton AA water where 100lb bags have been taken on several occasions.

Sorting out the best roach swims is difficult as there are so many of them. The right bank above Stourport, for instance, contains many excellent roach holes where outstanding catches have been made on tares. Winterdyne too, although much shallower, yields big catches occasionally. As for chub, they are just about everywhere, though if you're after big ones try the bottom end of Ribbesford. One of the most famous chub pitches on the river is the 'sunken boat' peg on the Lyttleton AA water, but though it is often full of chub, getting them out is very difficult and the sunken boat must be festooned with smashed tackle. Those big bream at Ribbesford—the shoal is usually somewhere in the area opposite the roadside café—also smash tackle. The fish, which range between 3lb and 9lb, are frequently tempted with legered breadflake. Most big hauls are taken from the left bank on the Dudley AS stretch, though it is also possible to catch them from the BAA water on the right bank.

The right bank below Bewdley Bridge is free fishing as far as Lax Lane where the Kidderminster DAA take over again. This KDAA length is the well-known Winterdyne waters and

An angler lands a small chub from a tree-lined far bank swim at Hawkesbatch, near Bewdley

extends to a small stream at Ribbesford Road which also marks the beginning of the Birmingham AA's Ribbesford fishery. The BAA stretch continues for $\frac{3}{4}$ mile to the boundary notice-board of the Lyttleton AA water. Day-tickets for the Lyttleton length which extends to the caravan-site below Stourport Bridge are issued on the bankside by a patrolling bailiff, except at weekends when it is reserved for contests. Contest bookings are available through the secretary.

On the left bank, immediately below Bewdley Bridge, is a short stretch of free fishing as far as the houses and factory. Kidderminster DAA leases the next length at Wribbenhall which runs from the factory to the caravan-site. Dudley AS control the water from here to well below Blackstone Rock. Club membership may be obtained through the secretary but there is a waiting-list to join, and the club do not issue day-tickets. The Stourport Power Station club lease the next short stretch as far as the boat moorings above Stourport Bridge. From here to the confluence of the River Stour below the bridge, is controlled by Stourport Council, and fishing where available (boats are moored in this area) is free.

Stourport to Holt Fleet

(See map page 166)

Steady and even-flowing, with depths varying considerably from 4ft to 15ft out in midstream, the river between Stourport and Holt Fleet contains plenty of small fish as well as big ones. Apart from the area around the confluence of the River Stour and below Lincomb Weir, there is little change in the speed of the current so it is ideal float-fishing water. Chub, roach and dace are the main species though there are barbel and bream scattered at various points. Below Stourport Bridge, roach and dace fishing can be first-class throughout the season and is excellent from autumn onwards.

Downstream of Lincomb Weir (famous for salmon), chub come more into the picture though the other species are still very much in evidence. On the left bank at Winnalls, chub to 3lb are taken on breadflake or casters trotted down the middle, while legered meat is another favourite method that brings big catches in winter. Winnalls is a famous contest water that yields remarkable catches when conditions are right. It is particularly good winter fishing and a firm favourite when the river elsewhere is virtually unfishable. Below Winnalls, deeper water attracts bream and there are several shoals of quality fish between Boreley and the weir above Holt Fleet. The stretch immediately below the weir is literally full of big chub and those fortunate members of The White Swan Piscatorials AC, who control it, think nothing of hauling in catches of up to 80lb.

On the left bank, the local Power Station Club (tickets from Mr M. Storey, Fishing Tackle Shop, Sutton Road, Kidderminster) control the fishing from the confluence of the Stour to the timber yard where the Goodwill AC take over as far downstream as the top of Lincomb Lock. Goodwill AC issue day-tickets at the waterside, and tickets to fish the Lock cutting can be obtained from the keeper. Private water extends from the bottom of the Lock to 150yd below the tail of the island where the Severn-Trent Water Authority have 500yd. This is free to licence holders but is not available between 1 February and 15 June. The following meadows are private as far as the start of the Kidderminster DAA Winnalls fishery which, apart from a short break, extends for 2 miles from the meadow above Hampstall Ferry to the bottom of Lady Ham Meadow. The remainder of the left bank is private as far as opposite the Lenchford Hotel where the Birmingham AA take over.

The BAA stretch runs downstream with a break at Lincomb Lock to within 25yd of Holt Fleet Bridge. Tickets to fish the Lock can be obtained from the keeper. Below Stourport Bridge, on the right bank, fishing is controlled by Lyttleton AA (day-tickets) for $\frac{1}{4}$ mile. The BAA take over at the boundary of the Lyttleton water for $\frac{1}{2}$ mile. This stretch, known as Newhalls Meadow, extends to Redstone Rock, which also marks the start of the Severn-Trent Water Authority's Lincomb free fishery (free to licence holders). This extends to a notice-board above Lincomb Weir and is closed from 1 February to 15 June.

More Authority water begins at the hedge at the tail of the island and continues to the upstream boundary of the Hampstall Hotel water—day-tickets, including salmon, from the hotel. Below the boundary of the Hampstall Hotel water, the fishing is private as far as two meadows above Holt Fleet Weir where The White Swan Piscatorials AS (members only) take over down to the bridge.

170

Holt Fleet to Worcester

(See map page 166)

Apart from the stretch immediately below the weir at Bevere, the Severn is very steady in this area though the depth varies considerably. Wide in places and with steep banks in parts, this is one of the most improved lengths of the river. A large head of small fish, but also plenty of big ones, provide excellent sport and several experts predict it will be even better in the next few years. Bream especially are on the increase as small skimmers are now caught at most venues. Bigger ones too, turn up at odd spots usually in the deeper holes, and many bags of 50lb to 60lb have been landed by pleasure anglers over the last two or three seasons.

Chub are found all along the reach but usually where the banks are tree-lined or bushy and, though the majority are on the small side, two- and three-pounders are quite common. One of the best chub haunts of the Severn can be found at the upstream end of the Blackheath AC stretch. Here, below the weir at Bevere, 100lb catches are not unusual in summer and autumn, while the 'rubbish hole' as the locals call a pitch near the weir, dominates the club's many contests. Roach too thrive along the Bevere stretch. Many small 2oz and 3oz roach are caught throughout the season from all parts, which augurs well for the future.

Dace are quite prolific on some stretches, and bleak seem to be everywhere. Barbel also appear to like this part of the river as many are taken from the upstream area. They are good-sized fish too, ranging between 4lb and 6lb. Generally, tactics for this reach depend on the depth close in. Up to 10ft calls for float-fishing, middle river style, that is a heavy stick float or balsa supporting casters tripping the

171

bottom. This method will attract all species, though in deeper water (and it sometimes runs up to 14ft at the rod end) a sliding float is a better proposition. When the float fails, legering or the swimfeeder pays dividends, especially for the bream and barbel which are often out in midstream.

On the left bank, the Fleet and Wharfe Hotels have day-ticket water below the Holt Fleet bridge which is followed by a long length of private water controlled by the Fleetman AC and The White Swan Piscatorials. Blackheath AC waters commence at the meadow above Bevere Weir and continue for 2 miles to Northwick Lane below Barbourne. Membership is open through the secretary. Hazeldine AA lease the adjoining Severn Meadow and Newheys Hill waters. Membership is through affiliated clubs or the secretary. A short private length comes next and then fishing is free from the top of Pitchcroft racecourse to the bridge.

The right bank for three meadows below Holt Fleet Bridge belongs to Worcester DUAA. This Association leases many miles of the Severn in the Worcester area and membership is open to anyone. The next two meadows, known as the Holt Castle waters, are controlled by Mr F. J. Harper who issues permits. Birmingham AA have the next 2 miles. This Grimley fishery extends to a point above Bevere Weir and island. The next length, with the exception of the lock cutting, is owned by the Camp Hotel which issues day-tickets, for four meadows boundaried by a cottage. The lock cutting can be fished on permits obtainable from the lock-keeper. The BAA's Hallow waters commence here and extend for 1½ miles to the start of a short piece controlled by Worcester DUAA. The Worcester stretch ends at Hallow tip and then the water is free, where accessible, as far as Worcester Bridge.

The Clevelode caravan park (members only) controls the next length, and then several small private stretches follow as far as Cliffy Wood. This is the upstream boundary of the Malvern AA waters which continue for 1½ miles. A small private stretch comes next followed by Hanley Castle AC water (members only). This extends to Poole Guest House and fishing is reserved for guests as far as the caravan park. Below the park, at Upton Brook, is the start of Upton AA's water which stretches to Upton Bridge. Day-tickets for this piece and another stretch below the bridge are issued on Mondays to Fridays, and at weekends if no contests are booked. Permits can be obtained from the local tackle supplier Mr Geoff Shinn. Membership of the club, subject to the committee's approval, is open through the secretary.

Worcester to Upton-on-Severn

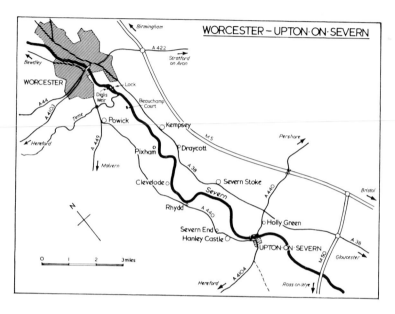

Even-flowing, quite wide and, with depths of up to 15ft out in the middle, there is little variation in the river between Worcester and Upton. Two outstanding features, however, are the weir at Diglis and the confluence of the River Teme on the right bank further downstream. The Teme, a great game river, often influences the quality of sport for several miles below where it enters. For instance, if the Severn is low and stale, the Teme water tends to bring the fish on feed, while if the Teme runs in high and badly coloured it puts them off. The weir at Diglis is one of the top salmon beats on the Severn, and the bank below is usually lined with anglers throughout the salmon season.

The main species along this reach are chub, roach and bream, though there are one or two shoals of barbel, plus

174

plenty of dace and the usual multitudes of bleak in all parts. Generally, the fishing is somewhat patchy hereabouts, and though there are many excellent stretches there are also plenty of mediocre lengths. Often too the fish seem to prefer one bank to the other, so if the right bank is good the left bank is poor or vice versa.

The roach fishing has improved in recent years with big catches coming from many areas. The left bank immediately below Worcester Bridge, is good roach water as far downstream as the Cathedral. East Diglis produces big bags also, as does the top of Beauchamp Court, the 'trees' opposite Kempsey Church, Clevelode, Oak Meadows and parts of Severn Stoke. Tares or casters in summer and autumn, and bronze-coloured maggots in winter bring the best results.

Chub are plentiful in most areas, though as on other parts of the river, the tree-lined stretches bring the best sport. The area around Teme mouth is a famous chub haunt, as is the 'trees' length at Beauchamp and the top end of Clevelode. Other 'chubby' spots can be found at Oak Meadows on the left bank, Severn Bank House above Upton, and anywhere on the right bank from Clevelode to Upton. Float-fished casters usually bring the biggest hauls, but legered meat is a firm favourite among many top match-anglers.

Although the river in this area supports a large head of bream, they don't show in any quantity above Clevelode. There is one well-known 'hot spot' near the access track at Beauchamp Court, and 'skimmers' are caught on the mud-flats above Pixham Ferry, but otherwise you have to go downstream from Clevelode to find them. Popular bream haunts such as the 'oak tree' at Clevelode, Latham's Farm at the bottom of Oak Meadows, Severn Bank House opposite the cliffs at upstream Severn Stoke, and in the trees downstream of the access road at the same venue, all produce big catches when conditions are right.

The left bank below Worcester Bridge is controlled by the Ecclesiastical Commissioners but is considered free fishing as far as the Diglis locks. Worcester DUAA's East Diglis

175

fishery begins below the lock and extends for $\frac{3}{4}$ mile. The following meadows are private as far as the Severn-Trent Water Authority's Kempsey water (free to licence holders) which runs down to the Severn Yacht Club. Below the Club, at Kempsey Church, is the start of Kempsey AA's water which stretches for $1\frac{1}{2}$ miles. Membership is open through the secretary. A short private length follows the Kempsey water, and then Worcester DUAA take over again for 3 miles. This is the Oak Meadows water and it extends to Latham's Farm. The Worcester DUAA boundary marks the beginning of the Birmingham AA's Severn Stoke waters which, apart from a short gap in front of Severn Bank House, extend to Upton Bridge.

The right bank from Worcester Bridge to Diglis Weir is controlled by the Severn-Trent Water Authority who also hold the salmon rights below the Weir. Worcester DUAA take over at the bottom of Weir Lane for four meadows which extend to one meadow above Teme mouth. From here on downstream is private until Beauchamp Court where Worcester DUAA take over again. This lengthy stretch continues to the bottom of Clevelode. A small day-ticket stretch (tickets from Mr Little) in the village adjoins the Worcester DUAA water and extends to the high bank which is inaccessible.

Upton-on-Severn to Tewkesbury

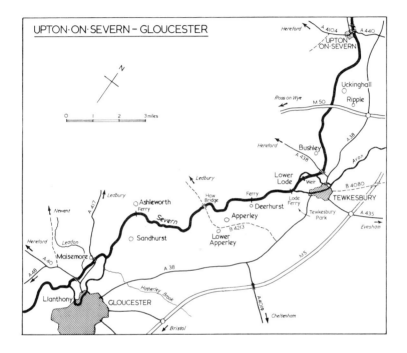

With depths of between 18ft to 20ft in places, this is the deepest and slowest moving stretch of the river. Bream, roach and chub are the main species, though there are hordes of bleak in virtually every swim. In fact these voracious little fish are so thickly spread that it is often difficult to get a bait through the shoals and down to the river-bed with float tackle. Dace are plentiful in parts, and barbel turn up occasionally but they are too few to make it worthwhile fishing for them. Small eels are everywhere and these can be as much a nuisance to the leger fisherman as bleak are to the float angler.

In recent years, huge carp have been caught in the Upton

177

area. These fish, which range up to 20lb, appear to like legered luncheon meat, as local tackle-dealer Geoff Shinn can verify. Geoff has caught several with this bait. He reckons the carp entered the river when the Marina was dug out from an old pool adjacent to the river. But wherever they came from the carp are now well-established.

The roach fishing at Upton is some of the best on the river, and bags of 50lb plus are taken frequently through summer and autumn on tares and hempseed. Later on, bronze-coloured maggots come into their own. The best roach swims at Upton are along the right bank below the Bridge, where close-in tactics bring results. Roach figure at many other spots along this reach, however, usually where the depth is no greater than 8ft, though they sometimes pick up baits offered for bream in deeper water out in mid-river.

Bream are prominent at most venues from Upton downstream. The first 'hot spot' is the area around the old railway bridge. Many big hauls have come from here, including two Severn Championship winning catches taken on breadflake. At Bushley, the bream 'hot spots' are on the bend opposite Uckinghall, upstream of the motorway bridge, the area around the BAA car park, and near the windmill towards Mythe Bridge. Along the left bank, they can be found at Uckinghall, Ripple—above the motorway bridge—opposite the car park at Bushley, and above Mythe Bridge. Legering well out is the most popular method—the swimfeeder works well here too—though good bags are made close in where there is a good depth, say 12ft or over.

The chub population has increased remarkably in recent years and they are caught in most swims. The best spots, however, are where the banks are tree- or bush-lined. Unfortunately, the Severn-Trent Water Authority's engineers keep chopping the trees down, and several once well-known chub swims are now no more. Most chub are taken fairly close in on the float—plenty of lead shot is needed to get the bait down quickly, and often the depth demands a slider —though legered luncheon meat and swimfeeder also bring good results.

The left bank immediately below Upton Bridge is private as far as the Marina. Below the Marina, Upton AA have a short length for members only. The next 1,000yd are inaccessible because of the high bank, and then follows two short private stretches before the start of the Birmingham AA's Uckinghall water. This extends for one mile to below the ferry at Ripple. The next length, which continues beyond the motorway bridge, is controlled by the Severn-Trent Water Authority. More BAA water continues from here to Harris Court. Then follows private water as far as the confluence of the Avon below Mythe Bridge. Tewkesbury Popular AA have the next length from the Mill to the confluence of the Mill Avon below the weir. Day-tickets are issued through the secretary and fifty outside members are allowed.

The right bank, below Upton Bridge, is free down to the end of the houses where Upton AA take over for 1,000yd. The Severn-Trent Water Authority control the next length which extends to the old railway bridge. The BAA's Bushley water starts here and continues uninterrupted for $3\frac{1}{2}$ miles to Mythe Bridge. Below the bridge is private for a short distance; and then the BAA take over again for a further $\frac{1}{2}$ mile.

Tewkesbury to Gloucester

(See map page 177)

Below Tewkesbury Weir the Severn is tidal, yet to the inexperienced eye there is little change in the character of the river as it flows down to Gloucester. It is perhaps a little wider in places and the colour is a shade heavier at normal level, but the banks remain tree-lined and green with none of the bare mud-flats normally associated with tidal stretches. Neither is the water brackish or saline. In fact, as far as angling is concerned, the only effect the tide has, is on the river's flow and colour. Certainly, the fish population is unaffected as chub, bream, roach, dace, bleak, pike and even the odd barbel continue to provide good sport. Eels are more numerous, as one would expect, but an added bonus is a fair head of carp ranging up to the 14lb mark which turn up regularly in the higher reaches. Flounders too are quite common along the whole of the length.

The way in which the tides influence the flow depends on the height and the amount of fresh water in the river. In general it can be said that tides below 26ft are stopped by the weir at Llanthony, near Gloucester, and their only effect is to slow the river down. Above 26ft however, the tides top the weir and the effect is quite dramatic in that the river comes to a standstill before flowing in the opposite direction. At the same time it rises very rapidly—as much as 2ft to 3ft in a few minutes—which can be quite dangerous to the unwary. In more detail, and taking the high-water-mark at Sharpness, the following rules apply on a normal level river. At Ashleworth, small tides begin to take effect about $1\frac{1}{2}$ hours after the peak at Sharpness, and rise for half-an-hour. Big tides arrive in just over half-an-hour and rise for an hour. At Lower Lode, small tides arrive $2\frac{1}{4}$ hours after high-water at Sharpness and big tides in an-hour-and-forty-minutes—the rise-time being the same as Ashleworth. Small tides, which merely slow down the flow, are welcomed by anglers as the fish often feed much more freely at such times. They also take baits more readily as the river is becoming more lively under the influence of a big tide. But as soon as it begins to flow in the opposite direction, before running off at a fast rate, fishing is often hopeless for 3 hours or more due to the speed of the current and the large amount of mud and silt suspended in the water. Nevertheless, there are long periods between tides when the river flows quite normally and these can easily be determined with the aid of a tide-table sold by many tackle dealers in the area. For instance, if the peak of a big tide comes at 8 a.m., the river is back to normal by noon and remains so for about 8 hours until the next tide. Because of the constant wash of the tides, the depth varies considerably even in localised spots along the whole length. The average is between 11ft to 14ft in the deeper parts, but sometimes there is as little as 4ft close in.

The depth generally determines the sort of fish found in a particular swim and, as along the non-tidal length, the bream prefer the deeper water which is usually (but not always) well out in midstream. Tactics for bream are the same as those used above Tewkesbury, but because of the eel problem it is asking for trouble to throw in large amounts of maggots. Cereal groundbait, plus a few casters, is better, though maggots can still be used on the hook. The other species are caught fairly close in and the ideal swim is between 6ft to 7ft deep. The best method for these swims is float-fished casters or maggots with loose feed as an attractor. Not much lead is required to get the bait down to the bottom. In fact, the normal middle river style works fine.

Roach are prolific at many venues, especially in the Haw Bridge area, and bags of up to 70lb were taken on tares in the summer of 1976. Stewed wheat is another useful bait for roach in these parts though it has lost some of its appeal in recent years.

181

The carp are usually hooked by bream anglers legering breadflake, but have also been known to grab maggots and casters offered by float-anglers. Many, of course, are lost on frail tackle but enough are landed between Lower Lode and Haw Bridge to suggest that they might well become a specific target in the near future. The weir pool itself yields large bags of chub and barbel, as well as pike, eels, salmon and shad. Below Gloucester the river is always heavily coloured and the only serious angling is for eels and flounders.

The left bank from the weir to the Mill Avon confluence is leased by Tewkesbury Popular AA (see Upton to Tewkesbury). Gloucester United AA then have a lengthy stretch which extends to Deerhurst Church. Day-tickets are available in advance and membership is open through the secretary. The boundary of the Gloucester water marks the beginning of the Birmingham AA's Deerhurst holdings which extend to Apperley. Then follows a short private length before the start of Gloucester UAA's Haw Bridge stretch. This commences one meadow above the bridge and continues to within one meadow of the confluence of the River Chelt. The area above and below the Chelt confluence is owned by the Red Lion Inn, Wainlode Hill, which issues day permits. From the boundary of the Red Lion water downstream fishing is private.

On the right bank the BAA have a long length which starts on the dead arm of the Severn at Upper Lode Lock and continues for 2 miles with a gap at Lower Lode Hotel. At Chaceley, the Yew Tree Inn controls a short stretch (day-tickets available), then the BAA take over again as far as the Avon Sailing Club. Below the sailing club, Hazeldine AA have two meadows and adjoining this is Gloucester UAA water which extends to below Ashleworth Quay. The remainder of the right bank, to where the river divides, is privately controlled. At Maisemore the BAA have five meadows with a gap on each side of the lock.

Appendices

1 Licences

All anglers are required by law to have the appropriate Regional Water Authority licence to fish. Licences for the Severn, which run from January to December or for 28 day periods, are sold at all tackle dealers in the Severn catchment area. Concessionary (cheap) licences for juniors between 12 and 15 years of age, registered disabled persons, and senior citizens, cost 30p. Salmon licences are obtainable for one day or a full season. Concessionary salmon licences are issued for juniors, disabled and senior citizens.

Seasons:
Freshwater fish: From 16 June to 14 March.
Trout: From 18 March to 30 September.
Salmon: From 2 February to 30 September.
Eels: It is lawful to fish for eels with rod and line during the annual close season for freshwater fish.

Restrictions:
Fishing with a float is forbidden in the close season for coarse fish. Cereal and maggot baits are also barred in the same period. Keep-nets for retaining fish cannot be used during the close season. Size of keep-nets should not be less than 1.5m in length. Rings should not be less than 35cm in diameter or, if rectangular, less than 35cm x 23cm. Mesh size should not be more than 15mm.

2 The Birmingham Anglers' Association

The Birmingham Anglers' Association own outright or rent scores of miles, probably well over a hundred, of the Severn from Llanidloes to Gloucester. Membership is open to anyone through an affiliated club or as an associate, and there are different categories covering coarse and game fishing or both. Salmon fishing is not available to associate members. The cards are as follows:

Club Coarse Cards
Membership through an affiliated club covering coarse and trout fishing but not on waters designated 'Fly Only'.

Club Coarse and Trout Cards
Membership through an affiliated club covering coarse and trout fishing including 'Fly Only' waters.

Club Salmon Cards
Membership through an affiliated club covering coarse, trout and salmon fishing with the restriction that not more than 15 per cent of any club's members (excluding associate members) may hold these cards.

Associate Coarse Cards
Individual membership covering coarse and trout fishing but not on waters designated 'Fly Only'.

Associate Coarse and Trout Cards
Individual membership covering coarse and trout fishing including 'Fly Only' waters.

Associate Junior Cards
Individual membership for junior anglers aged between six and sixteen covering all coarse, trout and salmon waters.

Birmingham AA waters are listed in the membership book but full details and maps are given in the Association's *Guide to Waters.* Further information can be obtained from BAA HQ, 40 Thorp Street, Birmingham B5 4AU.

3 Clubs, Associations and Societies

BIRMINGHAM AA:
HQ, 40 Thorp Street, Birmingham B5 4AU.

BEWDLEY AS:
Secretary, J. Evans, Lawnswood, Highley, Bridgnorth, Salop.

BLACKHEATH AC:
Secretary, John Green, 73 Regis Road, Rowley Regis, Warley, West Midlands.

BRIDGNORTH AS:
Secretary, D. Michel, 47 Danesbridge, Well Meadow Estate, Bridgnorth, Salop.

BRIDGNORTH COMRADES
c/o Secretary, Listley Street, Bridgnorth, Salop.

BRIDGNORTH ROYAL BRITISH LEGION AC:
c/o Secretary, Bridge Street, Bridgnorth, Salop.

CHESHIRE AA:
Secretary, Dick James, 34 Sweet Briar Crescent, Crewe, Cheshire.

COVENTRY DAA:
Secretary, M. Williams, 134 Scots Lane, Coundon, Coventry.

CREWE AMALGAMATED AC:
Secretary, Club HQ, 9 Beech Street, Crewe, Cheshire.

CREWE PIONEERS AC:
Secretary, J. Meyler, 11 Lengfield Drive, Crewe, Cheshire.

DAWLEY AC:
Secretary, Keith Brown, 26 Severn Way, Little Dawley, Telford, Salop.

DITHERINGTON (Shrewsbury) AS:
Secretary, J. Almond, 35 Sundorne Crescent, Shrewsbury, Salop.

DUDLEY AS:
Secretary, A. R. Dalwood, 4 Warrenhall Road, Dudley, West Midlands.

GLOUCESTER UNITED AS:
Secretary, P. Farnsworth, 10 The Butts, Newent, Glos.

HAZELDINE AA:
Secretary, J. W. Hazeldine, 8 Dudley Road, Sedgley, Dudley, West Midlands.

IRONBRIDGE AC:
Secretary, Bert Wilcox, 23 The Wharfage, Ironbridge, Salop.

KEMPSEY AA:
Secretary, B. Davis, 8 Elm Court, Elm Close, Worcester.

KIDDERMINSTER DAA:
Secretary, M. Millinchip, 246 Marlpool Lane, Kidderminster, Worcs.

KINVER FREELINERS AC:
Secretary, R. Oliver, 68 High Street, Kinver, Staffs.

LEIGHTON SAC:
Secretary, Bert Wilcox, 23 Warfage, Ironbridge, Salop.

LIVERPOOL AA:
Secretary, J. Johnson, 97 Liverpool Road, North Maghull, Liverpool.

LLANIDLOES AC:
Secretary, D. Davies, Mount View, China Street, Llanidloes, Powys.

LMS AC (Shrewsbury):
Secretary, J. Thorpe, 13 Hordley Avenue, Heath Farms, Shrewsbury, Salop.

LYTTELTON AA:
Secretary, Ivor Cooper, 64 Mostyn Road, Stourport, Worcs.

MALVERN AA:
Secretary, Mr Dalley, 59 Beauchamp Road, Malvern Links, Malvern, Worcs.

MONTGOMERYSHIRE AA:
Secretary, Rev. Robin Fairbrother, The Vicarage, Bettws, Newtown, Powys.

PRINCE ALBERT AS:
Secretary, C. Sparkes, High Lodge, Upton, Macclesfield, Cheshire.

PROVINCIAL AA:
Secretary, W. Hunt, 11 Central Avenue, Bilston, West Midlands.

RABY ESTATE OFFICE:
Uppington, Telford, Salop.

ROLLS-ROYCE AC:
Secretary, Derek Flower, 1 Windermere Road, Shrewsbury, Salop.

SABRINA AC:
Secretary, W. G. Smart, Sunnyhill, Lyth Bank, Bayston Hill, Shrewsbury, Salop.

SEVERN-TRENT WATER AUTHORITY:
Fisheries Office, 139 Church Street, Malvern, Worcs.

SHIFNAL AC:
Secretary, G. Howells, 4 Coppice Road, Shifnal, Salop.

SHREWSBURY AND ATCHAM COUNCIL:
The Guildhall, Shrewsbury, Salop.

SHROPSHIRE ANGLERS' FEDERATION:
Secretary, P. Moody, 65 Broadway Avenue, Trench, Telford, Salop.

SHREWSBURY AS:
Secretary, Gerry Williams, 14 Allerton Road, Harlescott, Shrewsbury.

ST HELENS RAMBLERS:
Secretary, J. Prestcott, 76 Birchley Street, St Helens, Lancs.

TELFORD AA:
Secretary, K. Burgess, 22 Elm Park Drive, Wellington, Telford, Salop.

TEWKESBURY POPULAR AA:
Secretary, R. Smith, 10 Trelawn Gardens, Pyke Farm, Tewkesbury, Glos.

UPTON AA:
Secretary, R. Webster, 8 Furlongs Road, Upton-on-Severn, Worcs.

WARRINGTON AA:
Secretary, S. Jackson, 2 Nora Street, Warrington, Cheshire.

WHITE SWAN PISCATORIALS:
Secretary, R. G. Dutton, 8 Rushbrook Drive, Parklands, Sutton Coldfield, West Midlands.

WHITMORE REANS AA:
Secretary, H. R. Hughes, Star Chambers, Princes Square, Wolverhampton, West Midlands.

WORCESTER DUAA:
Secretary, R. Coley, 71 Woodman Rose, Droitwich, Worcs.